MEXICO

MEXICO

ARCHITECTURE · INTERIORS · DESIGN

MARK LUSCOMBE-WHYTE

DOMINIC BRADBURY

FOR MARIE

Front cover design based on a pattern by Manolo Mestre, used at
Casa Luna, Careyes (see page 106), which was itself modelled on
an Aztec symbol of a bird of paradise.

First published in 2003 by
Conran Octopus Limited
a part of Octopus Publishing Group
2–4 Heron Quays, London E14 4JP
www.conran-octopus.co.uk

Publishing Director: Lorraine Dickey
Executive Editor: Zia Mattocks
Editor: Emma Clegg

Art Director: Chi Lam
Art Editor: Alison Fenton
Artwork Illustrator: Russell Bell

Production Manager: Angela Couchman

British Library Cataloguing-in-Publication Data
A catalogue record for this book is available from the British Library

ISBN 1 84091 319 3

Printed in China

CONTENTS

Map labels: San Diego, Tijuana, El Paso, USA, Chihuahua, Brownsville, Monterrey, GULF OF MEXICO, La Paz, Victoria de Durango, Mazatlán, Tropic of Cancer, San Luis Potosí, Tampico, Las Pozas, Chichén Itzá, Cancún, Mérida, Isla Cozumel, PACIFIC OCEAN, San Miguel de Allende, Guanajuanto, Guadalajara, Puerto Vallarta, Úxmal, Cobá, Campeche, Morelia, Teotihuacán, Barra de Navidad, Careyes, Colima, Toluca, Mexico, Manzanillo, Pátzcuaro, Puebla, Veracruz, Cuernavaca, Valle de Bravo, Ixtapa, Palenque, BELIZE, Acapulco, Oaxaca, Monte Albán, San Cristóbal de las Casas, Puerto Escondido, GUATEMALA

CULTURE & DESIGN

Mexico is a land of masks, mirrors and illusions, as its storytellers and poets so love to remind us. As a country – and a vast, epic, extraordinary country – it defies all definitions, expectations, generalizations and stereotypes. What might be true of parts is seldom true of the whole; such is the intoxicating diversity of Mexico.

This place of shadows, opposites and contradictions has 31 states that make up the Estados Unidos de Mexicanos. These states envelop desert and rainforest, smoking-gun volcanoes and trembling earth, jungle canopies and deep-fissure canyons, agricultural tablelands and smoking geysers, striking coastlines to the east and west and great mountain ranges sweeping into the skies. 'It isn't one country,' writes Carlos Fuentes, Mexico's greatest contemporary novelist, in *The Death of Artemio Cruz*, 'It's a thousand countries with a single name.'

In landscape and cityscape, the scale and drama of Mexico can be overpowering. In our imagination it might sometimes be overtaken by its endless neighbour to the north, yet we should not forget that Mexico is four times the size of France and the second-largest country in Latin America. This is a place of great, invigorating journeys holding countless revelations. It is startling to think that this country was once twice the size, before New Mexico, California, Arizona, Texas and other territories were ceded to the United States in the mid-nineteenth century.

No wonder that Mexico has often been bound up with ideas of utopia. For the Spanish conquistadores who arrived in force in 1519 under Hernán Cortés, 'New Spain' as they called it was often described as a paradise – although, as they soon realized, this was an unforgiving paradise peppered with dangers and temptations. For Cortés and his followers, Mexico was a place where they might realize the dreams of power and wealth that had brought them from the Old World. For some who traced the footsteps of Cortés, like the brutal Nuno Guzmán, the hunt for gold and power was an obsession, centred on the hunt for the mythical El Dorado.

Yet for every Guzmán and his order of black disciples there were idealists such as Vasco de Quiroga, or 'Father Vasco', the missionary who followed in the terrible wake of Guzmán, trying to right his wrongs and

LEFT (CENTRE) *A gardener in the organic fruit garden store room at the Cuixmala estate in Jalisco: one of the many faces of Mexico.*

CLOCKWISE FROM TOP LEFT *A market seller stacking prickly pear at Mercado Abastos, Mexico City; farmers savouring an early morning shot of pulque near Teotihuacán; a mariachi in Mexico City; a religious procession by the church of Atotonilco, near San Miguel de Allende; a mobile sales team selling tupperware near Mérida, in the Yucatán peninsula; and a stall holder taking a siesta at Mercado Abastos.*

the English author D H Lawrence looked to the Indian culture for enlightenment and hoped to found his own utopian society, dubbed 'Rananim'. He failed, of course, but you can visit his grave a little farther north, near Taos, New Mexico, where he still lies – a stone's throw from his ranch. Edward James, an eccentric English writer, amateur architect and patron of the arts, built a vast jungle folly in San Luis Potosí, a day's drive from the Texas border. This was another personal paradise, a free expression of his own creativity and desires. Others include Graham Greene, Edward Weston, Malcolm Lowry and Gabriel García Márquez – Mexico has long been a haven and inspiration to writers, travellers and artists.

The idea of building a utopia also found expression in the architecture and design of New Spain. As well as offering a place where visitors might find what was lacking in them or their homeland, Mexico as a place of promise also meant liberty of expression and a chance to build afresh. Colonial architects and artisans laboured to create something familiar, but also something new. Some bathed in an artistic freedom that was unthinkable in Europe, where the demands of social expectation, patrons and fashion limited their every move. Mexico presented a dramatically different context, as well as a strange set of materials and influences … and the example and skilled craftsmanship of the Mexican Indians themselves.

A strange fusion of blood, influences and themes resulted in a character, temperament and style in Mexico unlike any other. From the moment the conquistadores arrived, they relied on their alliances and relationships with the Indian population to expand their power; controlling such a vast territory would have been impossible without them. This was the start of a complex two-way process of social interchange, as well as the beginning of a great *mestizo* culture – a people sharing Spanish and Indian descent. Unlike in many other colonial territories, where indigenous Indians and their communities have been marginalized, in Mexico an initial reliance on the Indian world and the development of what is now a natural *mestizo* majority has meant that Indian culture

build communities based on the model of Sir Thomas More's *Utopia*. Tolerating Indian traditions within the fold of the Catholic Church, supporting human rights and founding missionary schools and hospitals, Quiroga and his kind were the benevolent, paternal face of the Conquest. Bartolomé de Las Casas, who became bishop of Chiapas, or the 'Protector of the Indies', also fought colonial excesses in Mexico – as he had elsewhere in the Americas – and struggled to create utopias of his own.

Ever since then, Mexico has had a strange allure for dreamers and romantics. In the early twentieth century,

and tradition is, on the whole, treated with respect. In Mexico, Montezuma II and his cousin Cuauhtémoc, the last Aztec Indian kings toppled by the conquistadores, are as honoured as Cortés, if not more so.

For the Spanish, the Mayan people of the Yucatán peninsula were their first contact with Mexican Indians. In 1517 Francisco Fernández Córdoba, a slave dealer supplying Spanish Cuban haciendas, was pushed off course by storms so his ships landed on the Yucatán. He was welcomed at present-day Campeche but along the coast half his men were killed and Córdoba was wounded. He made it back to Cuba, and the governor, Diego Velazquez de Cuellar, sent an expedition back to the Yucatán in 1518 under Juan de Grijalva, who then christened the country New Spain. Cortés himself travelled from Cuba, heading a larger expedition ordered by Velazquez. He first landed on the island of Cozumel and began to explore the Yucatán, helped by a Spanish sailor, Gerónimo de Aguilar, who had been shipwrecked in 1511 and had been living with the Mayans ever since.

'The houses in those parts where there is stone are of masonry and mortar and the rooms are small and low in the Moorish fashion,' wrote Cortés of the Mayan towns. 'In those parts where there is no stone they make their houses of adobe, which are whitewashed and the roofs covered with straw. There are houses belonging to certain men of rank which are very cool and have many rooms, for we have seen as many as five courtyards in a single house … And the temples … are the largest and the best and finest built of all the buildings found in the towns; and they are much adorned with rich hanging cloths and featherwork and other fineries.'

The conquistadores could not help but be impressed by the achievements of Mayan culture, despite the fact that most of the great Mayan cities and temples – such as Chichén Itzá, Uxmal and Cobá, with their dramatic pyramidal towers towering over the flat jungle canopy – had long been abandoned. Cortés and his people arrived hundreds of years into the decline of the Mayan civilization, which had been at its peak during the period

AD 700–900. Some cities had been taken and burnt by rival Indian groups, but others were abandoned for no clear reason; the Mayan disintegration is still an enigma.

At its height, the Mayan empire spread across the Yucatán peninsula into neighbouring Belize, Guatemala and beyond. But even today there are as many as five million Mayan speakers in Mexico and Meso-America. Many Mayan Indians in the Yucatán and Chiapas still live in traditional oval, wattle-and-adobe huts of the kind Cortés describes, with thatched roofs and a single, central front door. The Mayans were not only highly accomplished architects, but masters in sculpture and weaving, fresco painting and pottery. They were astronomers and scribes, employing hieroglyphics to create codices and histories, and their cities are wonders of the ancient world.

Now the Mayans are among as many as 24 million Indians across Mexico, accounting for perhaps 30 per cent of the total population, including the Zapotec, Huichol, Mixtec, Nahua, Purépecha, Chinantec, Huastec and Yaqui peoples. They have their individual languages

ABOVE *Farmers outside a small chapel off the road from Atotonilco to San Miguel de Allende, with cacti towering behind them.* LEFT *An adobe village hut near Atotonilco in Guanajuato state. Without care, such homes have a limited lifespan as the sun that bakes the adobe bricks will eventually crack the mud and turn it to dust, while rain also erodes the fabric of the house. Adobe has become something of a rarity as modern and more enduring materials have taken over, although contemporary architects and designers are leading a revival of interest.*

and cultures but share much in common; some remote communities have never embraced the Spanish language and continue to isolate themselves from the excesses of the contemporary world.

Collectively, Indian Mexico remains a vibrant ark of skilled craftsmanship, creativity and invention. Each culture has its own frame of reference, its own themes and concerns, its own specialities, partly dependent on its surroundings and the materials to hand. But there is also a long and valuable history of textiles, ceramics, metalwork, woodwork and stonemasonry, much of which is recorded through the murals and codices formed by the Mayans.

Weaving and embroidery have long been the preserve of women, and their story is partly told in traditional dress: the wrap-around pleated skirts seen across much of Mexico in rainbow colours; the *huipil* sleeveless tunics and dresses, often in white cotton but embroidered around the neck and collar; the *rebozo,* or shawl, also seen across the country but in a huge variety of fabrics, colours and motifs. Cotton and agave fibre have been widely used and spinning, fixed looms, back-strap looms, embroidery and (from the colonial era onwards) lacemaking all have common currency. In some parts of

Chiapas, women are buried with spindle, needle and thread so that they can attend to their dress on the long voyage through the afterlife.

Ceramics, too, have a noble pedigree with a history stretching back thousands of years. From more functional pieces such as water storage jars, pots and dishes, to ceremonial objects such as funeral urns and idols, and more ornamental elements such as figurines and pieces of jewellery, Mexican pottery has a colourful and varied past. Vintage ceramics glazed with figures and legends tell age-old stories to archaeologists and historians. And this is still a land of potters: recent and contemporary artists such as Teodora Blanco, Aurelio Flores, Jorge Wilmot and Herón Martínez Mendoza have continued the ongoing reinvigoration and evolution of Mexican ceramics.

Together with frescos, murals and other traces of pigment and pattern that were once used to decorate pre-Hispanic temples and buildings, Mexico's textiles and ceramics constantly remind us that it has always been a country of colour. Most famously there is cochineal, the strong, secure red pigment that is obtained from the sun-dried or toasted husks of tiny insects of the same name, which thrive on certain kinds of cacti and prickly pear.

The colonialists were taken aback by the vibrant colour of cochineal, which had long been used as a dye by the Zapotec Indians and others.

Based in Oaxaca, the Spanish cultivated the cochineal industry using Indian expertise. They began to export cochineal back to Europe on the 'cochineal fleet', supplying colour by the ton in pellets mordanted, or fixed, with lime juice, alum or salt. These shipments became second only to Mexican-mined silver in value, and Spanish exporters and importers guarded the secrets of cochineal production closely, cultivating an alluring mystique that only increased the appetite and fashion for its use. In the 1770s a French spy, Thierry de Menonville, went to Mexico to learn the secrets of cochineal, or 'Spanish Red' as it was sometimes called. He went to Oaxaca, where much of the old town – including the great church and convent of Santo Domingo – had been built on the profits of this sun-drenched, inferno-like shade, and succeeded in smuggling samples of the insects out of the country.

But there were, of course, many other natural colours. Yellow came from turmeric roots and lichens, orange from annatto tree berries, black from logwood found in the swampy areas of southern Mexico and Belize. Indigo was widely used, especially by the Mayans, who fixed it with clay and used vivid blues in frescos. Even their sacrificial victims, it is said, were coated in indigo before they left the mortal world and stepped over, with blue footprints, into the afterlife.

The Mixtec Indians on the southern Pacific coast of Oaxaca had their own version of the imperial purple manufactured by the Romans from molluscs in North Africa. Like the Romans, the Mixtecs milked *purpura pansa,* or sea snails, for a lilac dye, as it was considered bad luck to kill them. The Spanish christened it 'New World Royal Purple'. Now the industry has all but faded away, just like cochineal production to the north.

These colours had an immense impact on the conquistadores, on Spanish merchants and entrepreneurs, and on Europe, where art itself was revolutionized by access to a host of new, stable, vivid natural colours,

which could be adapted and mixed to yield a wealth of tones and shades. They would also make their way into the murals and frescos of churches, cathedrals and the domains of the wealthy, often those who had grown rich on their investments in the New World.

Yet of the most famous and once most powerful of Indian cultures very little now remains. The vast Aztec empire, centred upon a 'Triple Alliance' between the city states of Tacuba, Texcoco and Tenochtitlán – the latter forming the Aztec capital – once stretched from coast to coast. The Aztecs, or Mexica, arrived in the Valley of Mexico right at the very heart of the country in the early fourteenth century. Within this valley, surrounded by

ABOVE *A street corner in the historic town and port of Campeche in the Yucatán peninsula. Many of the buildings in the old town of Campeche – grouped around the central square, or zócalo, and Cathedral – are painted in bright, vibrant colours.*

ABOVE LEFT *The vast citadel of Teotihuacán, north of Mexico City, once housed a quarter of a million people and dates from the fourth century BC to the seventh century AD, when it was abandoned. The Aztecs later used Teotihuacán as a ceremonial centre.*

ABOVE CENTRE *Tenayuca, north of Mexico City, is one of the few surviving Aztec-built sites.*

ABOVE RIGHT *Across the Yucatán peninsula the Mayans constructed monumental cities like Chichén Itzá; from the Temple of the Warriors and the reclining figure of Chac Mool, the eye is drawn to the central castle.*

RIGHT *Remnants of Monte Albán, west of Oaxaca, formerly the capital of the Zapotecs. Strategically positioned on a dusty hilltop, the site offers views right across the Oaxacan valley.*

hills and mountains, was a lake system formed by water trapped within the volcanic rock that formed an epic basin; here the Aztecs founded Tenochtitlán.

By the time the conquistadores arrived in 1519, the Aztec empire had grown under warrior kings such as Montezuma I and Ahuitzotl, supported by a system of alliances and accommodations. Tenochtitlán itself had become a great city: it was built upon the old lake beds, was surrounded by water and set within a Venetian-style environment with a complicated arterial map criss-crossed with canals, waterways, causeways, bridges and floating gardens and fields.

One of the countless contradictions within Mexican history was that the Aztecs were both highly sophisticated and shockingly brutal. Their capital must have been quite extraordinary – much larger and more accomplished than most European cities of the day. Among the many temples, shrines and palaces stood the central Templo Mayor, or Great Temple, dedicated to Huitzilopchtli, the god of sun and fire, and Tlaloc, the god of rain and lightning. Aware that the city was slowly sinking into the old lake bed, the Aztec architects and engineers used a lightweight volcanic stone for the core of the walls of the temple and then faced it with basalt and heavier stones, which were also used for stairways and towers.

Templo Mayor and its precinct were enlarged from time to time and the completion of every phase was marked by mass human sacrifice: hearts were torn out and flung into ritual bowls and blood flowed down the steep ranks of steps. A warrior people, the Aztecs would sacrifice their prisoners of war, who would go willingly, believing themselves blessed and chosen by the gods for a place in the heavens. King and nobility would begin these mass sacrifices and then, worn out, would hand over to the priests, whose noses and ears were lacerated and their bodies marked by ritual scarring. In times of drought the Aztecs would even feel a duty to offer their own children for sacrifice to please the gods and bring the rains. It was believed that the tears of their mothers and fathers would have to fall before the clouds could open.

Despite the horrors perpetrated because of the Aztecs' beliefs, based on a complicated pantheon of gods, the Aztecs were at the same time sensitive, intellectual and erudite. Art, artistry and architecture were of great importance, as was poetry. In addition to Templo Mayor and the august palaces of kings and the nobility, Tenochtitlán had a great library holding the Aztec codices, not to mention gardens, aviaries and a zoo.

Montezuma II, who came to power in 1502, was a typically severe leader, and an elitist, but also a just man. He was intelligent and devout and, importantly, obsessed with necromancy and omens. He was troubled by the meaning of comets and eclipses, which he believed warned of disaster. When his lookouts sent back paintings of Cortés and the conquistadores with their horses, canon and guns, he thought a prophecy had come true.

Aztec legend told of Topiltzin Quetzalcoatl, a serpent god who slept with his sister in a drunken stupor and fled over the eastern sea to the red lands in shame. One day he would return as 'the white hero of the break of day'. Cortés, to Montezuma, seemed like a returning god.

The epic story of Cortés, Montezuma and the conquest of Mexico is extraordinary: the building blocks of camp-fire stories, an almost biblical tale of friendship and betrayal, struggle and victory. Montezuma nervously welcomed the conquistadores into his city and they were amazed by what they saw. Bernal Díaz, a conquistador who travelled and fought with Cortés, wrote an accomplished and moving account of the Conquest in which he describes the approach to Tenochtitlán and its later destruction:

'When we saw all those cities and villages built in the water, and other great towns on dry land, and that straight and level causeway leading to Mexico, we were astounded. Those great towns and cues and buildings rising from the water, all made of stone, seemed like an enchanted vision from the tale of Amadis. Indeed, some of our soldiers asked whether it was not all a dream ...

'... The sight of the palaces in which they lodged us! They were very spacious and well built, of magnificent stone, cedar wood, and the wood of other sweet-smelling trees, with great rooms and courts, which were a wonderful sight, and all covered with awnings of woven cotton.

'When we had taken a good look at all this, we went to the orchard and garden, which was a marvellous place both to see and walk in. I was never tired of noticing the diversity of trees and the various scents given off by each one ... Everything was shining with lime and decorated with different kinds of stonework and paintings which were a marvel to gaze on ... I stood looking at it, and thought that no land like it would ever be discovered in the whole world ... But today all that I then saw is overthrown and destroyed; nothing is left standing.'

An uneasy friendship moved to violence and then to the death of the great appeaser, Montezuma, and the Spanish fleeing Tenochtitlán during the fabled *Noche*

Triste. The Old World clashed savagely with the New as the iconoclastic conquistadores, newly reinforced by compatriots, laid siege to the city; in 1521 the last emperor, Cuauhtémoc, led the Aztecs to their place in history.

Cortés was one of the great Machiavellians; his achievement was immense, whatever the cost. He won an unknown, unmapped country through fierce determination, in the face of intense hardship, fear and danger, as well as risking the wrath of the Cuban governor and King Charles V for exceeding his authority. And the Aztecs, wrote Octavio Paz, the Mexican nobel laureate, in *The Labyrinth of Solitude* 'suddenly lost sight of their destiny. Cuauhtémoc fought in the knowledge that he would be defeated ... and his people died alone, abandoned by their friends, their allies, their vassals and their gods. They died as orphans.'

Cortés and his successors began to lay the foundations of a new city, the capital of New Spain, upon the ruins of the old. The Aztec temples and palaces were

LEFT AND ABOVE *The ornate, multi-coloured interiors of the Sanctuario de Guadalupe in the city of Morelia. The church itself is early eighteenth century, while the ornate interiors were conceived in the early twentieth century by Joaquín Horta Menchaca, using baked clay and a vibrant palette of paints. The arresting paintings depict scenes of the arrival of the Catholic faith in Mexico and the conversion of the Indian people.*

torn down and the stones used to begin building colonial New Mexico. The oldest cathedral in Latin America, Mexico Cathedral was begun in 1525 and stands right alongside the ruins of Templo Mayor.

The growing ranks of colonialists pushed their territory northwards and westwards with expeditions hunting for gold and silver. The discovery of silver in the north led to a mining boom – a Mexican rush – which helped the expansion of New Spain. Cortés was honoured with the title of Marqués de Valle de Oaxaca and rewarded with granted estates. He fought with King Charles V against the Ottoman Turks in 1540, a disastrous battle at Algiers, and seven years later he died in Spain, all but forgotten.

New Spain, by then, had a momentum of its own. El Dorado had proved elusive but the mines were working, run on Indian labour, and rich land enabled the beginnings of the hacienda system. Missionaries followed in the wake of the conquistadores, spreading the gospel and building churches, schools and hospitals. The Indians took to Catholicism with unexpected acceptance, as though it filled up a vacuum created by the Conquest itself. The transition between Indian pantheons and the Catholic faith was aided by similarities: notably the emphasis on ritual, penance, baptism, blood symbolism and martyrdom. Symbols such as the Mayan cross, representing the Maya's Tree of Life, would have a resonance to both faiths, with links with the underworld and the heavens.

Church and colonial state alike adopted Spanish and European architectural styles, creating a *mélange*, in the sixteenth century at least, of Gothic style, Spanish classicism and also Mudéjar, or Hispano-Moorish, architecture. The very last Moorish province in Spain, Granada, had fallen as late as 1492 – the culmination of La Reconquista – so to many of the conquistadores and the colonialists, Moorish architecture was something very real and familiar. Cortés and Bernal Díaz constantly described Mexican Indian temples, ceramics and decoration as 'Moorish', which might sometimes simply translate as exotic. But to the architects of New Spain, Mudéjar was part of their palette, as they began to stamp their own personality upon their work. The architecture of older Mexican cities such as Campeche or Morelia is often reminiscent of the Moroccan style: central courtyards, Moorish arches, even zellige tiles climbing the walls.

Yet, as Indians applied their own creativity to their labours and the *mestizo* population began to grow, elements began to fuse and to create something Mexican. In more remote areas, especially, a missionary with no architectural prowess would build a church with Indian craftsmen and labourers, armed with typically no more than a postcard or a drawing of a Spanish cathedral or church. The results were an interpretation of Spanish style with elements of Indian and *mestizo* experience.

This fusion of Mexican culture had a strong life blood. Missionaries tolerated and even encouraged the co-mingling of beliefs and influences to ease the shift into Catholicism and a new way of seeing the world. On 9 December 1531, 12 years after the Conquest, a dark-skinned Virgin (just like an Indian or *mestizo*) appeared to an Indian peasant on Tepeyac Hill, north of Mexico City, as he made his way to Mass. The Virgin of Guadalupe became known as the Empress, the Madonna of Mexico: she was its patron, its saviour, its mother (despite her similarities to the Iberian Virgin of Guadalupe from Extremadura, who was a figurehead for Spanish soldiers fighting the Moors and heading off to the colonies). Now she is the great emblem of Mexican

liberty and freedom, with her adopted and adapted image everywhere. 'The legend gave the Indian self-respect,' wrote Graham Greene. 'It gave him a hold over his conqueror; it was a liberating, not an enslaving, legend … The Virgin of Guadalupe, like Saint Joan in France, had become identified not only with the faith but with the country; she was a patriotic symbol even to the faithless …'

The Day of the Dead, too, is a powerful co-mingling of Indian and Catholic concepts. For the Mexican Indians, this day was an annual celebration of death when the souls of the departed would return to them. It was celebrated after the rains in November, when the scent of marigolds and wild flowers helped the dead find their way from the underworld to the mortal plane. It fitted in with the whole Indian, and now Mexican, attitude to life and death, which saw them as two sides of the same coin. Death is as natural and as familiar as life. Seeing the power of this festival, the Church did not try to undermine it, but simply merged it with All Saints and All Souls to create a two-day celebration second only to Holy Week, which is the pinnacle of the Mexican calendar.

The festival has now become much diluted, confused with Mexican ideas of fiesta and even the American theme of Halloween. But around Lake Pátzcuaro in Morelia can be glimpsed a more authentic vision of the Night of the Dead and the Day of the Dead. In some villages, still, the first day of November is thought of as the day of the angels, when lost children are remembered. Then comes the Night of the Dead, when families gather together in the village cemeteries around the decorated graves of their loved ones. At midnight the deceased visit their living family and they spend the hours until dawn sharing time with them. It is a communal, life-affirming celebration, with children, mothers, fathers and grandparents all coming together.

Some weep, some smile and some sleep amid the darkness as the candles flicker on the graves, alight with the colour of magenta cockscomb and marigold petals, while a meal of *pan de muertos*, or bread of the dead, fruit and drink honours the dead. A church bell tolls in the distance, guiding the visiting souls. The decoration has become a source of pride in itself, some taking photographs of the graves that they have adorned and tended. At dawn on 2 November the spirits depart. People pack up their blankets and food and go back to their homes as Mexico wakes and starts to commemorate the Day of the Dead in a thousand different ways.

This fusion culture and life philosophy filter into all aspects of design, artistry and architecture and make their way through the centuries. Adobe mixes with stone and Moorish arches, images of the Virgin of Guadalupe decorate the walls of a Mayan wattle-and-thatch hut, Indian motifs and colours define the fabrics decorating a town house in Campeche or Veracruz, which looks as though it has been lifted from the streets of an Andalusian Spanish city. On the Pacific coast a contemporary *palapa*, or palm-thatched home, is filled with colonial antiques.

Throughout the years and within an often troubled history that included a war of independence in the early nineteenth century and the Revolution and accompanying civil war of the early twentieth century, other influences also added to the powerful intermingling of architectural and stylistic elements. In the 1860s, in the face of an economic meltdown, the Mexican government suspended repayment of foreign debts, giving Napoleon III of France an excuse to invade Mexico. The French were famously defeated by Mexican troops at Puebla on 5 May 1862, a victory still celebrated with an annual holiday. But a year later the French, determined to build an empire in the Americas, took control of Mexico and installed Ferdinand Maximilian von Habsburg, Archduke of Austria and a cousin of Queen Victoria, as emperor of Mexico.

The famous rule of the young Maximilian and his wife Charlotte Amélie, or Carlota, daughter of Leopold I of Belgium, was brief and inglorious. They arrived in Mexico City in 1864 showered with flowers and installed themselves in the former residence of the Spanish viceroys, Chapultepec Castle. By 1867, pressured by the Americans and facing a Prussian threat in Europe, Napoleon pulled out his troops. Maximilian was shot and Carlota lost her

LEFT AND ABOVE *Only Holy Week outdoes the Day of the Dead in importance in the Mexican calendar. Spectacle, adornment and adoration combine in honouring the dead, as graves are tidied and decorated with candles, wreaths and flowers, here in villages around Lake Pátzcuaro, Morelia. All kinds of imagery have become bound up with this festival, with the Virgin of Guadalupe and the figure of Christ honoured along with family loved ones. In homes special altars are prepared for honouring the dead, often bearing photographs of the departed and layered with food and a few of their favourite things. On the Day of the Dead itself, a Mass is sometimes said in the graveyard (far left, below).*

ABOVE *Detail of a house in Mexico City designed by Legorreta & Legorreta. The work of Ricardo Legorreta, perhaps the best known of all contemporary Mexican architects, is celebrated for its use of intense colour, geometrical forms and a strong relationship between the outside and the inside.*
RIGHT *Luis Barragán's sculptural Satellite Towers of 1957, designed in collaboration with the artist Mathias Goeritz, stand between the highways in a borough on the edge of Mexico City. The five concrete towers symbolic of a growing skyline – the highest 50 metres (54 yards) tall – suggest the common alliance between architecture and art in modern Mexican design.*

mind. Yet Maximilian had presided over a brief fashion for Francophile architecture and design and struggled to bring some formal order to Mexico City, which was already growing into a city of chaos and sprawl. In 1864 Maximilian began remodelling his palace and ordered the construction of Paseo de la Reforma – or Calz del Emperador as it was known at the time – Mexico City's key artery and one of the few reliable ways for strangers to navigate this colossal city. Carlota arranged for a double row of eucalyptus trees to be planted along its borders.

Despite the cautionary tale of Maximilian and Carlota, thirty years later French style was again all the rage. The 34-year dictatorship of Porfirio Díaz, the *Porfiriato*, was a pre-revolutionary time of peace, wealth and indulgence, bank-rolled by the profits of mining, sisal and tobacco production and a wave of foreign investment. European styles of dress, architecture and living became very fashionable, with cafés and theatres emulating the Parisian model. Mock-Tudor houses and French villas sprang up like mushrooms in the affluent suburbs of Mexico City and French-trained architects such as Emilio Dondé were much in demand. Art Nouveau was very popular in parts of the city, such as Colonia Roma and Juarez. Díaz himself, so passionate about encouraging foreign money and manners into Mexico, would end his days in exile in France.

But after the Revolution, which began in 1910 and launched a sad decade of internecine conflict, Mexico looked for something different. There began a gradual rethinking of Mexican architecture and design, which included a look back to pre-Hispanic architecture – the pyramids, patios and ziggurats of Mayan cities especially, as well as indigenous *pueblos* and adobe homes. Two strands of twentieth-century architecture and design began to emerge. One was largely internationalist, heavily influenced by what was happening in the United States and the example of the pioneering Modernists. The other, more focused on Mexican identity, but with access to the tools and materials of Modernism, was best exemplified by Luis Barragán, the godfather of contemporary Mexican

architecture. His work was suffused with a striking modernity, yet it drew upon the traditional forms and colours of Mexican towns and villages.

Today it is hard to say whether Mexican architecture is experiencing a second renaissance or whether we are simply seeing a continuation of the process that was begun by Barragán and others. The breadth and energy of the country's approach to design is obvious and inspirational, as this book will testify. Statesman architects such as Ricardo Legorreta and Teodoro González de León have created landmark buildings in Mexico and carried the message of Mexican design to a wider international market. A younger generation of designers, notably Manolo Mestre, Héctor Velázquez Graham and José de Yturbe, continue to reinterpret familiar elements of Mexican architecture in original and vibrant ways and nurture a spirit of experimentalism.

There are common elements and strands that run through Mexican architecture and design today: the importance of nature, context and landscape; the use of colour and texture; the strong relationship between design and art. But diversity and invention is as important now as it ever was, bringing constant surprises.

There has always been a sense in which Mexico has stood at a crossroads: between north and south, east and west, between two kinds of America, the New World and the Old. In the colonial era ships would come from the Far East laden with textiles, spices or ceramics and unload at Acapulco. These would then be transported overland and sent to Europe. Something similar happened in the other direction as ships arrived in Veracruz filled with the latest that Europe had to offer. Mexico is still at the crossroads – and is all the better for it – between ancient and modern, between simplicity and sophistication. 'We love mystery and surprises,' says Ricardo Legorreta, Mexico's most influential contemporary architect. 'Even in our way of being we are rather mysterious. We say we are a simple people but we are extremely complicated. The depth of the architecture we create is the depth of Mexico and its people.'

COLONIAL

Architecture is bound up with identity. The design of buildings acts like a mirror, reflecting the values, concerns and aspirations of a people; it is the outward face of a society. So from the days of the destruction of the Aztec civilization and the victory of Hernán Cortés and his conquistadores, New Spain was destined to change. Cortés and his followers saw the symbolic need to tear down the walls of the old Aztec cities and temples, whose sacrificial horrors had so appalled the colonialists' sensibilities, and build a new image over them, reflecting instead Spanish, European and Catholic traditions. Mexico Cathedral was built alongside the wreckage of Templo Mayor, while the Basilica of the Virgin of Guadalupe in Tepeyec, on the edge of modern-day Mexico City, was built on another sacred Aztec site.

Essential to the development of this New Spanish architecture and to the pacification of the Indian people was the conversion orchestrated by the Catholic Church and its missionaries. As the early Spanish Crown *audencias* and viceroys laboured to expand, understand and organize the fruits of the Conquest, the missionaries presented the more acceptable face of colonialism. The Franciscans began arriving in the early 1520s, just a few years after Cortés, including the Apostolic Twelve who walked the long, difficult road from Veracruz to Mexico City barefoot. They, and the Dominicans who followed, were admired by the Indians for their devotion, propriety and sense of self-sacrifice. By the end of the sixteenth century, across Mexico there were as many as 160 Franciscan convents alone.

'The flight of their gods and the death of their leaders had left the natives in a solitude so complete that it is difficult for a modern man to imagine it,' writes Octavio Paz in *The Labyrinth of Solitude*. 'Catholicism re-established their ties with the world and the other world. It gave them back a sense of their place on earth; it nurtured their hopes and justified their lives and deaths.'

'Thanks to religion,' he points out, 'the colonial order was not a mere superimposition of new historical forms, but a living organism. The Church used the key of baptism to open the doors of society, converting it into a universal order open to everyone.'

The missionaries founded not only churches and convents, but hospitals and schools. Later, Church and state would clash repeatedly – before and after independence – over the power and wealth in the hands of the Catholic fold in Mexico, but during the sixteenth and seventeenth centuries the missionaries were there to offer protection and paternalism. This was embodied not only in the friars and the clergy, but in the churches themselves, with their borrowed influences from Spain and Rome.

Dominican buildings tended to be straightforward and simple. The Franciscans were prolific builders and occasionally ornamental, while the Augustinians favoured

PREVIOUS PAGES (LEFT) *A statue of the Virgin Mary at Hacienda Poxilá (see page 46), near Mérida on the Yucatán peninsula.* (RIGHT) *A view of the colonnade and courtyard at Mahakua, Hacienda de San Antonio, Colima.*

LEFT *A lily seller by a church fountain in San Miguel de Allende. The walls of the church are painted in a typically Mexican shade of red; given the history of cochineal in the country, red seems one of the most authentically and naturally Mexican of colours.* ABOVE *Lighting votive candles in a church near Oaxaca; a horse tethered at Hacienda Uayamón in the state of Campeche; and a street scene from San Miguel de Allende.*

ABOVE *El Sanctuario de Atotonilco, near San Miguel de Allende, with a lathe nave and six chapels. The interior is adorned with poems and eighteenth-century frescos by a local artist.*

a more exuberant expression. From a mixture of Gothic and Mudéjar elements in the sixteenth century, the influence of the Renaissance showed through with a more classical approach. Architectural styles passed through the filter of skilled Indian craftsmen and artisans who interpreted them under the guidance of the missionaries and secular clergy. *Parroquias*, or parish churches, were built as best as materials and labour allowed.

El Sanctuario de Atotonilco, northwest of San Miguel de Allende, for instance, was founded in 1740 as a place of penance and retreat and is now seen as one of the wonders of Mexico. The breathtaking frescos on the ceilings and walls are those of a local Indian artist, Miguel Antonio Martínez de Pocasangre. Father Miguel Hidalgo y Costilla, hero of the independence movement, stopped here with his small army of insurgents to raise the banner of the Virgin of Guadalupe as a symbol of Mexican liberty.

From the 1650s onwards the famous predilection for Mexican baroque started to take hold, initially in Mexico City, and began to swallow conservative classicism.

The decorative flamboyance of the baroque mirrored the devotion of the growing congregations. Structural elements in the form of columns, archways and cornices began to disappear under a flurry of colourful ornamentation, partly funded by the large endowments pledged to the church from those made wealthy by mining, cochineal or hacienda agriculture. Elaborate façades and altarpieces, such as the Capilla de los Santos Angeles in Mexico Cathedral, are masterpieces of baroque excess.

'Among us,' wrote Carlos Fuentes in *A New Time For Mexico*, 'the baroque is a necessity, a vital, resounding affirmation of a necessity. A devastated, conquered land, a land of hunger and of dreams, finds in the baroque the art of those who, having nothing at all, want everything.'

In the eighteenth century this baroque flamboyance was taken a step further with the introduction of the Churrigueresque style, a hymn to decoration and colour at its apex in the late-baroque *estípite*, an inverted pyramid design used for altars, and sometimes façades, in a riot of brightly coloured garlands, saints, angels and cherubs.

It was almost inevitable that there would be a reaction to this artistic excess, and it came in the politically troubled nineteenth century with the arrival of Neo-classicism. In many Mexican churches baroque flourishes were removed and destroyed, partly within an anti-clerical reaction against the institutions of the Church itself, which had come to be regarded as corpulent and indulgent.

This architectural evolution, loosely following the tides of European fashion but incorporating skills and passions all of its own, was also reflected in the development of colonial cities such as Veracruz, Morelia and Campeche. Most of them adopted European grid-like street systems with a *zócalo* or central square, usually with the cathedral or town church on its edge. Domestic architecture did not adopt the same baroque excesses, but decorative flourishes were introduced in the use of colour, tilework, panelling and carved masonry. The character of towns was partly determined by the kind of materials to hand; Morelia, for example, is called the 'The Pink City' after the volcanic stone used in its buildings.

Out in the countryside the haciendas acquired a character of their own. These were the great agricultural estates that emerged in the early days of New Spain, granted by the Spanish Crown to the conquistadores, colonial powerbrokers and administrators, and worked by Indian labour. Some were vast territories – one hacienda in Chihuahua to the north was larger than Belgium. No two haciendas were completely alike, but they shared many similarities and tended to have either a symbiotic relationship with a neighbouring village or form villages or small towns all in themselves, sometimes with their own hospitals, schools, dormitories, churches or chapels, prisons and stores. Often the workers would not be paid in cash but were expected to trade the value of their labour at the hacienda store.

These rural estates were arable-based, but the Spanish also introduced the farming of cattle and sheep on a large scale. At the same time a significant equine culture developed. A love for the horses which the first conquistadores brought with them, and which frightened Indian villagers who had never seen one in their lives, seeped into the Mexican *mestizo* character. Most haciendas had large stable blocks and rodeo grounds; some even had their own bull rings.

In the Yucatán peninsula the various styles of architecture used for the haciendas can be seen. Some, like Hacienda San José in the north, were concentrated around a large, open plaza and surrounded by a series of low-slung houses and buildings, including a chapel. San José dates from the early nineteenth century with cattle, corn and sugar its staples; in the 1880s Antonio Bolio Guzmán swapped his Teatro Bolio in Mérida for the hacienda. Farther south, in Campeche state, Hacienda Uayamón, the 'Place of the Tender Huayas', constituted a community all in itself with cottages for supervisors set to one side and the main house built into a hillside and reached via a sweeping set of steps climbing upwards to verandas and the entrance hall. Both, like a number of haciendas in the Yucatán peninsula and elsewhere, have recently been restored and converted into alluring hotels.

All over the peninsula the chimneys of old hacienda machine houses can be seen towering above the trees, like masts on a horizon. They mark the heyday of the region's haciendas at the end of the nineteenth century and the beginning of the twentieth when a mechanized way of extracting henequén fibre, or sisal, came into use. Most haciendas in the region expanded with the profits from this agave 'green-gold', used in rope and heavy fabrics. But within a decade the Revolution began the process of sweeping the haciendas away, continued by a wave of land reforms.

Many of the Yucatán's haciendas are still in ruins, some beyond repair, the grounds of the great houses now used as dusty football fields. Those such as Hacienda Granada, Santo Domingo and Kochol are falling apart. At Hacienda Chunchumil the colonial grandeur of the days of the *Porfiriato* can be seen. Here a guardian unlocks the doors of some of the surviving state rooms, where you can see fragments of chinoiserie on the crumbling walls and Art Nouveau stencils. Porfirio Díaz, the last president before the Revolution, stayed here in 1906.

ABOVE *Many of the vivid frescos were buried under whitewash until recently; they depict themes such as the Passion, devotion to the Rosary, and the Battle of Lepanto in 1571.*

LEFT *A stairway in the convent of Santo Domingo, which was established in the seventeenth century. The convent was occupied by Santa-Anna's troops in the 1820s and became a barracks once again during the 1860s after its friars had all but dwindled away. In the 1970s the building was restored as the Museum of Oaxacan Cultures and forms part of a complex that consists of convent, church, library and botanical gardens.*

RIGHT *The barrel-vaulted nave of the church of Santo Domingo, with a replica of the original high altar that was destroyed by troops in the nineteenth century. The church was reconsecrated in 1902 and later returned to the Dominicans. With the sensitive restoration work that has taken place, the church is widely regarded as one of the most glowing examples of the baroque across the whole of Mexico.*

SANTO DOMINGO

Saint Dominic's mortal name was Domingo de Guzmán. He was a Spanish priest who founded the Dominican order of preaching friars in 1215. This was one of the missionary orders answering the call to convert New Spain and layer Catholicism over ruined Indian temples, building solid, monumental churches and convents that would resist earthquakes and other natural forces. The external adornment on these buildings was concentrated around doorways and windows, although as the convent and church of Santo Domingo testifies, the interiors were a different matter.

The colonial jewel of Oaxaca, Santo Domingo was founded in 1570 and consecrated 40 years later, despite being damaged by earthquakes before it was finished. The architect is unknown, but it is thought that the design was conceived by the Dominicans themselves, with the façades of the convent in largely classical style, plus Gothic influences in some of the vaulted galleries. Built on a large scale, with cloisters looking out onto a vast central courtyard and fountain, the convent features some decorative flourishes such as a double staircase with elaborate stucco work.

Inside the church the feeling is even more theatrical, with a wealth of baroque stucco work and inset paintings of saints, prophets and biblical scenes. On the ceiling of the lower choir is the family tree of the Guzmán family – a literal tree in moulded, gilded and painted stucco with figures sprouting from the branches. The convent and the church have been sympathetically restored, with the former now a museum. The nearby botanical garden, filled with cacti and local planting, provides a soothing, natural contrast to the man-made baroque glories of Santo Domingo itself.

LEFT, RIGHT AND BELOW
The convent and church of Santo Domingo – circled by a beautiful series of cactus gardens – are a centre point for the annual Guelaguetza, or Lunes del Cerro, festival in Oaxaca towards the end of July. This festival of folk dancing and music begins with a costumed procession from Santo Domingo to the central zócalo. The Zapotec origins of the festival suggest the complex history of the town. This included the colonial exploitation of native skills in the production of cochineal red dye, which flooded the town with wealth and in its turn led to the generous endowments that made possible the building of Santa Domingo.

ABOVE, RIGHT AND FAR RIGHT The design of the staircase and hallways of the convent has been compared with the accomplishments of Spanish monasteries, such as Madrid's El Escorial. In the case of both buildings, the ornate depth of the stucco work and gilt is in contrast to the relative simplicity of the exteriors, which have a more obviously monastic, medieval quality. The convent is typical of the Dominican architectural style where buildings were solid and structurally relatively simple, but with decorative flourishes focused largely on stairways, doors and windows, with areas such as hallways and colonnades generally left unadorned.

ABOVE *A detail of the ceiling above the monumental main staircase in the convent of Santo Domingo. Such attention to detail, with the robes of the saints picked out in exquisite colours and in gold leaf, was not always typical of Dominican convent architecture in Mexico. Yet when they dedicated themselves to an idea, it was usually executed with precision and fine craftsmanship.*

ABOVE *The dome of the upper choir in the church of Santo Domingo illustrates the extent of the sophistication and achievement of both Dominican and Mexican artistry. The ranks of oval figures show Dominican saints and martyrs, while towards the centre the smaller images are of angels. The ceiling of the lower choir has a painted stucco family tree of Santo Domingo de Guzmán.*

HACIENDA TENEXAC

Giving the distinct impression of a fortress rising out of a dusty landscape, the Hacienda Tenexac has a dominating presence within its parched surroundings. In the state of Tlaxcala, not far from Puebla, Tenexac has been in the hands of the same Mexican family for hundreds of years. Almost untouched by the Revolution, which left so many haciendas in ruins, it is cared for and preserved by its current owner, the anthropologist and conservationist Dr Sabiro Yano Bretón, who works in the nearby town of Tlaxcala.

Tenexac was built in the eighteenth century and then restored in the late nineteenth century; originally its business was arable agriculture, then sisal and now it is cattle and bull breeding. As well as the *casa principal*, this was once a microtown with its own shop, chapel and school creating a self-sufficient, isolated community.

Dr Yano Bretón and his family have tried to keep the house much as it was, with its attractive fusion of European and Mexican elements. Some of the furniture is English, some French and some Austrian. The reception rooms, with family portraits lining many of the walls, feel as though they would not be out of place in London or Madrid, although from the outside there is a definite Andalusian or Moorish influence.

Today there are around 300 head of cattle at Tenexac and the estate is approximately 480 hectares (3,900 acres). There was a time in its past when Tenexac was seven times bigger, with its boundaries stretching off into the hills and towards the mountains in a harsh yet beautiful landscape.

ABOVE AND RIGHT *One of the great charms of Tenexac is its unspoilt and natural quality. Steeped in history, the house has been in the same family for generations (as suggested by the many family portraits and sepia photographs that line the walls in the reception rooms) and has been carefully looked after and preserved by its current guardians. Vintage touches such as the old telephone and the safe have been retained rather than swept away by modernization.*

RIGHT *It is interesting to see, in such rural locations, the contrast between simplicity and decorative flourishes in the design of haciendas. At Tenexac the simple castillo-like exteriors, made with locally quarried volcanic stone, and straightforward floor plans, are juxtaposed with fine wallpapers, wall stencilling and an eclectic collection of English, Austrian and French furniture gathered over the centuries. The drawing room (right) and dining room (below right) look much as they did a hundred years ago. There are no hallways – the reception rooms open into each other (below left).*

LEFT *Austrian tilework in the bathroom makes one think of the perilous journey such pieces must have made to find their way into a place where even the nearest town was once a day away on horseback or by cart. The European furnishings of many haciendas could be fiercely expensive to carry across sea and land and could take many months to arrive.*

ABOVE LEFT AND RIGHT *Religious icons and paintings find a place in most of the bedrooms, some of which are painted simply, while others have more ornate European-style wallpapers. The main bedroom (above), which has high ceilings with wooden beams picked out in cream and painted with a simple stencil design, features a large, canopied, four-poster brass bed.*

ABOVE *The* tienda *– or shop – of the hacienda, is lined with an impressive array of neatly partitioned wooden storage shelves. In many haciendas the workers were paid for their labour with food or goods from the store, or alternatively with vouchers that could only be redeemed there.*

LEFT *The tack room, including animal skins and an appropriately themed portrait, bears witness to the great importance of horsemanship and the* 'charro', *or Mexican cowboy, culture to the haciendas, especially those that were dedicated to cattle farming.*

Hacienda Poxilá

At the Hacienda Poxilá, just as with other haciendas in the Yucatán and beyond, there is a striking contrast between grandeur of scale and the relative simplicity of the architecture and decoration – a lack of pretension that lends these rural buildings much of their charm and beauty. Near the state capital of Mérida, Poxilá dominates a small, quiet village and its walls and buildings are painted a deep, sun-baked terracotta, edged with whitewash.

As well as the *casa principal*, or main house, there is an old machine house with its towering burnt-sienna chimney and wandering peacocks wisely taking advantage of the shade among the rusting cogs and winding gear. Narrow-gauge railtracks, which once carried trucks of sisal into the machine house, criss-cross the grass and lead you past outbuildings that were once used by workers and supervisors. On the other side of the *casa principal* and its front gardens, equine pursuits are catered for with stables and a riding ring.

The *casa principal* itself, sensitively restored by Poxilá's owner Alejandro Patron, is a cool oasis of calm, bordered by a series of terraces and *portales*, or long verandas, alongside the formal rooms of the house, all raised up at first-floor level. With parts of Poxilá dating back to the seventeenth century, but expanded in the nineteenth, the interconnecting reception rooms and library have been filled with an eclectic collection of artwork and icons, while colours mix primary yellow for the walls with blue for doors and shutters. Like so many haciendas, Poxilá has its own chapel with whitewashed walls, blue shutters, a terracotta tiled floor and three niches holding altarpieces.

LEFT At Poxilá the main reception rooms are at first-floor level – with some bedrooms and services below – allowing views of the garden and grounds from most of the main living spaces. This is also true of the many terraces and portales to both the sides and rear of the house. This long portale, topped with roof tiles imported from Marseilles, offers views across the grounds and towards the village church. At Poxilá, hacienda and village co-exist side by side, with the hacienda once supporting the villagers and vice versa.

RIGHT A view through to a central seating area at the front of the house. This room is open to one side, with a balcony overlooking the gardens and the front gates to the house. The breeze slides in and gently tips the rocking chairs, which shift and tilt as though worked by invisible strings. The paintwork and decoration of the hacienda is simple and charming, with the use of vibrant blues and yellows complemented by the cohesive terracotta floors throughout this part of the house.

LEFT The marble-topped desk in the study is perfectly placed for views of the front gardens and along a dramatic terrace stretching out to the side of the house. The study contains display cases with a collection of pocket watches and other curios.

BELOW The master bedroom on the first floor is a generous, cool space, with high ceilings and dramatic proportions.

LEFT AND ABOVE *The dining room, together with many of the other reception rooms, is home to a collection of icons and religious statues gathered from across Mexico. This large room with space enough for a dozen or more to dine is designed for entertaining, with the kitchen set off to one side. This part of the house has been lovingly restored, while nearby stands a defunct machine house (that was once used for extracting sisal) with narrow-gauge railtracks running out and into the estate. Not far off are the ruins of two Mayan pyramids, with water gardens close by.*

ABOVE Part of the exterior
of Hacienda Poxilá, with the
terracotta chimney of the old
machine house just visible
in the background.

RIGHT A simple ground-
floor verandah offers shade
and shelter from the sun.
Near the house there are
also stables and a riding
ring, adjoined by now-
empty bull pens.

LEFT *The simplicity of the chapel gives it power and elegance. This is a small family chapel, only for the house. The nearby village church, just a stone's throw away through the hacienda gates, provides a venue for larger gatherings.*

ORGANIC

'There was no denying its beauty, fatal or cleansing as it happened to be, the beauty of Earthly Paradise itself,' wrote Malcolm Lowry of the Mexican landscape in his novel *Under The Volcano*. And anyone who travels the Mexican countryside – even Lowry's ruined anti-hero Geoffrey Firmin – can hardly fail to be touched by the drama, seductiveness and fickle beauty of the country.

The conquistadores also wondered if this might just be paradise on earth; many who followed thought the same, albeit soon realizing that despite its beauty, it could also be unforgiving and suffused with the unexpected. The character of Mexico itself, including its attitude to life and death, is partly explained by this elemental and temperamental environment, or what Octavio Paz calls 'the indefinable threat that is always afloat in the air'.

From the expanse of the Chihuahua Desert in the north to the rainforests of the south, Mexico is a place of biodiversity and biospheres, providing unique habitats that attract artists and ecologists in equal measure. The landscape also inspires the architecture, which tends to rely on its surroundings for its building blocks and on nature for solutions to problems. Rural architecture and design, especially, have forged a strong relationship with the countryside and nature, experimenting with natural materials, colours and textures, with the reflections and sounds of water pools and fountains, while respecting the balance and themes of the surroundings.

Mexican organic architecture achieves its most obvious expression in the use of adobe. In North Africa it would be called *pisé*, in other parts of the world it might be called *cob*, but in Mexico and some southern American states, especially New Mexico, earth-baked architecture has a character all of its own. Adobe houses and *pueblos* were made of sun-baked earth bricks, then coated with a layer of rounded earth and lime plaster, which gives these buildings their sculpted, sensuous shapes.

Hive-like Indian *pueblos* survive near Taos in New Mexico, their walls thick and deep, offering a naturally cooled retreat from the sun. These *pueblos* are made up of interconnecting houses and stores, traditionally accessed from the roof by ladder (although doorways are now common), sometimes on one level but often with successive levels. Straw and stones would be added to the mud mixes to make the sun-dried bricks, helping to hold them together and also reinforcing the walls against the elements. As with any earth-based architecture, such homes are vulnerable to the hard climate, gradually drying out and crumbling in the sun, and being eroded by rainwater.

At Paquimé in northern Mexico, the ruins of a large adobe *pueblo* dating back to at least the thirteenth century can be seen. Adobe houses would originally have been built on one level, but as layer upon layer was added the town evolved to create a complex as many as five storeys high, supported by wooden beams, forming a skeleton

PREVIOUS PAGES (LEFT) *A donkey and cart in the countryside near San Miguel de Allende.* (RIGHT) *A waterfall at the jungle folly of Las Pozas, Edward James's extravagant and surreal wonderland in San Luis Potosí (see page 84).* LEFT *The old adobe walls surrounding Casa Reforma, the home of artist Sergio Hernández in Oaxaca (see page 78). The walls have been integrated into the design of the house, which has been built in a contemporary style, mixing adobe with glass, steel and other modern materials.* ABOVE *On and of the land: a farmer collecting corn outside Oaxaca; an agave field on the Pacific coast of Jalisco, a fine tequila state; and tending cattle near San Miguel de Allende.*

ABOVE *A pair of traditional, thatched Mayan huts in the Yucatán. These simple oval buildings are either constructed in stone, or with a wooden frame that is coated in sun-baked mud and mixed with straw.*

ABOVE RIGHT *The exterior of Piedra del Sol, designer Nicole Dugal's organic home – complete with palapa – on the Pacific coast north of Acapulco.*

over which the adobe stretches like skin. In the Yucatán traditional Mayan single-roomed houses are still made with tight, fence-like, vertical wooden frames, formed from lashed poles, to which a layer of mud is then applied, with a roof added in thatch.

Of course, adobe homes and churches were widespread across Mexico – especially in dry desert areas with little access to other materials such as wood and stone – and many still remain. But more contemporary, and less vulnerable, man-made materials have overtaken adobe as common currency, leaving it to a generation of younger, more innovative architects and designers to breathe new life into such an old technique.

Over the last 15 years, architect Héctor Velázquez Graham has been experimenting with adobe within his designs for contemporary houses in Mexico City, Oaxaca and elsewhere in Mexico. Much of his research has been to do with developing new recipes for adobe, which add bolstering materials such as concrete to the mud mixture. Such materials increase the lifespan and durability of the adobe bricks, which are made in wooden moulds and then sun-baked.

Making sure that the recipes are right and that the bricks solidify properly takes considerable experience and skill; if the sun isn't powerful enough or the air is too moist, the strength of the bricks will be compromised.

Adding pigments and different kinds of earth to the mix can result in a spectrum of earthy colours and tones.

'It's a beautiful material and a very Mexican way of expressing colour, texture and light,' says Velázquez Graham. 'We need to have an adobe made with quality ingredients and to work with people who really know how to build with it, as very few workers now have the skill … And it's not an easy thing to own a naturally made adobe house. It's like wood, which can last for a long time, but if you don't take care of it then it can become ugly and dangerous. The same happens with adobe. You take care of it, it will be beautiful. If not, it will melt away.'

Architect Sergio Puente, based in Mexico City, has also used adobe in a contemporary context, building houses down into the earth and landscape itself; he, too, had to train local builders to use adobe properly. In the Yucatán, architects such as Salvador Reyes Ríos have reinvented Mayan wood-farmed adobe huts as luxurious *casitas*, or little houses, reinterpreting traditional vernacular styles and adding a layer of modernity and comfort.

On the Pacific coast in the state of Guerrero, French-Canadian interior and landscape designer Nicole Dugal has worked closely with local artisans to create homes using hardwoods, palm wood, thatch and adobe. At Zihuatanejo in the north of Acapulco, she built a beach-front home for herself called Piedra del Sol in an organic style, mixing a sophisticated touch with vernacular elements such as the *palapa* – a wooden-framed, usually circular, thatched roof in an umbrella form covering rooms or terraces that are often partially open.

'These are simple constructions and it's what the locals know how to build,' says Dugal. 'The house is made with materials from the area, mostly wood that had already been felled and was left over from other houses. But if you want a crafted, authentic home, you have to wait until the artisans can come to you. Most of the year they are busy with their own homes, their farms, and for some of them building *palapas* or carpentry began almost as a hobby rather than a vocation. You can't expect to build houses like these overnight.'

Manolo Mestre adapts vernacular styles and organic materials to suit the location in which he is building: *palapa* for many of his projects on the coast, but in Valle de Bravo, a few hours' drive from Mexico City, he has used adobe and timber. 'I have always been interested in reinterpreting traditional architectural methods,' he says, 'and more and more I feel a compulsion to translate the vernacular into the contemporary; I don't like to be influenced by fashion.'

Like Mestre, José de Yturbe knew Luis Barragán and was much influenced by his work, noting his great respect for the landscape and the natural context of a building and creating spaces in sympathy with their surroundings rather than struggling against them. De Yturbe also works to emphasize the importance of gardens made in sympathy with a house's architecture and devotes his attention to landscaping and exterior features. His residential projects explore the relationship between interior and exterior, dissolving the boundaries and using terraces, patios and water elements to try to bring the world into a house and its inhabitants out into the world, while choosing carefully from a palette of regional materials and organic colours.

The real importance of rural living, and of the architecture of the countryside, has been dramatically enhanced over recent years partly by the massive growth of Mexico's cities, especially Mexico City, which has grown to an extraordinary mass of 20 million people; something like one in four of Mexico's population live in this, one of the largest cities in the world, and its many suburbs. Many of its wealthier inhabitants today seek refuge from the bustle and pollution in country escapes in Valle de Bravo and around Malinalco or Puebla, thus creating renewed demand for innovative rural homes that are bound to their environment.

Mexico has also always been a place for escapists of one kind or another. The great English eccentric Edward James created his surreal organic folly in the jungles of San Luis Potosí. The American artist James Brown has made a retreat for himself and his family in an old hacienda near Oaxaca, while Franco-German couple Veronique Lievre and Heinz Legler moved down from Los Angeles to the Pacific coastline near Puerto Vallarta to build another enchanting and remote country hide-away, accessible only by boat or foot. The siren call of the Mexican countryside remains difficult to resist.

BELOW *A detail of a new adobe wall at Casa Los Tres Helechos in Valle de Bravo (see page 64), designed by Manolo Mestre. A new generation of designers and architects have given life to such traditional materials as adobe bricks, interfaced here by pieces of clay tile that create a herringbone pattern between the bricks.*

VERANA

To reach Verana you need to take a 30-minute boat ride from Boca de Tomatlán, just to the south of Puerto Vallarta, until you reach the small fishing village of Yelapa, served by water taxis and mules because there are no roads here. Then there is a ten-minute walk up through Jalisco jungle pathways towards Verana, perched on a hillside overlooking the sea.

This a tranquil, intimate escape, founded and designed by husband and wife Heinz Legler and Veronique Lievre. Working in Los Angeles respectively as a film production designer and a set decorator, they wanted to create a personal refuge from the everyday world and here found the perfect location. Living in a tent nearby for a year, they called upon the skills of local craftsmen to turn their drawings and sketches into reality.

'We built it little by little,' says Legler. 'We were just building something for ourselves and as it evolved we started to think it might make a kind of hotel. We didn't know if it would really work or if people would be willing to come up here, so we tested it for a season. People really liked it.'

From modest beginnings Verana has grown to include six individual guest houses, as well as a jungle spa, restaurant, library and infinity pool slipping over the brow of the hills into the sea. Each house has its own unique character, drawing upon natural materials such as stone and wood. Each one's name suggests its flavour, including the Stone House, the Mayan House and the Palapa House. With its own mountain water source and a preference for oil lamps and candlelight, Verana is wrapped in an eco-conscious philosophy.

ABOVE *Like many of the guest houses, the Palapa House, built on two levels with stone floors, has a strong relationship between inside and out, with few solid walls and only the curving palapa offering separation and romantic enclosure. Billowing mosquito nets add to the exotic ambience. Beneath is a scene of the lily ponds amid the gardens of Verana.*

LEFT AND ABOVE *Both the design and décor of the Casa Grande are testimony to the eclectic, individual style of Heinz Legler and Veronique Lievre. They are collectors and flea-market hunters, mixing locally made pieces with others gathered from around Mexico and Los Angeles, where they spend part of the year. Here the red chair was found in a shoe store and recovered, while the 1950s cabinet on the wall was transported from Los Angeles.*

RIGHT *The exterior of the Casa Grande, with its private terrace, complete with Bertoia chairs brought back from Italy.*

ABOVE AND RIGHT *Various views of the Casa Grande, with its soft and relaxed colour palette. 'Each house represents a certain style,' says Legler, 'but they all had to look as though they had been here for many years.' A lot of the buildings made use of materials available locally, such as stone and bricks that were produced nearby. Water was another issue – a water source had to be located in the hills above and pipes laid to carry it down. 'Every morning someone has to make sure our tank is full and if not head up the mountain to see where the leak is.'*

ABOVE *The Stone House is home to a lamp from Pátzcuaro fixed on the wall and a locally made stool. The bed is from an antiques shop in Puerto Vallarta. 'We like finding things and turning them into nice pieces,' says Lievre.*

LEFT *The sliding wooden door in tirota wood is quite a weight. 'It was interesting getting it up the hill,' says Legler. 'A lot of things at Verana were actually made in pieces, transported here and then assembled here like a jigsaw puzzle.'*

LEFT *The choice of materials reinforces the organic quality of the house, especially the vast timber beams and stone fireplaces. Here the projecting roof partially protects the chimney terrace and part of the pool, which echoes the lake in the valley below. Large terracotta floor tiles up to seven centimetres (three inches) thick were specially made for the house.*
RIGHT *Light pervades the houses, casting shadows through spaces such as the hallway, which leads down to the bedrooms on a lower level, sunk into the garden.*

CASA LOS TRES HELECHOS

'I'm an architect who likes to work in the field, to draw on site, rather than at a draftsman's table,' says Manolo Mestre. This design of Casa los Tres Helechos in Valle de Bravo was very much a response to an especially stirring location. 'There was nothing there except a beautiful oak tree, so I wanted to create a homage to that oak tree by building the house around it.'

Located on a hillside that overlooks a lake and an old mining village, the house, with its four-gabled roof, was made of timber and adobe. Working according to organic-construction principles, the adobe mud was mixed with pine filaments and the gaps between the bricks were filled with pieces of the roof tiles that had been broken on their journey to Valle de Bravo, these forming a herringbone pattern between the smooth faces of the brickwork.

Given that the owners – the Mascarenas family – love to cook and entertain, to them the key part of the house is the combined kitchen and dining room, which opens on one side to the swimming pool and a chimney terrace, or loggia, partly sheltered by the projecting roof of the house. The family had to be encouraged to have a sitting room at all, but this now lies at the centre of the house, with its own large stone fireplace.

The connections between inside and out are vital, and so is the wealth of natural light. 'I wanted to design this timber structure as a free building,' says Mestre. 'The idea is that the windows almost seem to disappear, giving the feeling that you are floating in the middle of this beautiful, organic environment.'

LEFT *Built-in benches line one side of a breakfast table in a corner of the kitchen. The room was conceived as the heart of this home, as the owners love to cook, while a number of dining areas – inside and out – are dotted around the house. A local sawmill was used to source all the timber needed to build the house, giving it natural connections to its surroundings.*

ABOVE *The apex of the four-gabled roof makes a strong statement in the sitting room. The furnishings were a collaboration between Manolo Mestre and Eileen Mascarenas. The painting on the chimney is by Sergio Hernández (see page 78).*

ABOVE RIGHT *The sinks and counters in the bathroom are of volcanic stone, with hand-made bronze fixtures.*

RIGHT *One of the sunken bedrooms, sited on a lower level to the garden.*

CASA DEL SABINO

Mystery is important to José de Yturbe. He likes to create houses that don't reveal themselves in an instant and that don't wear their hearts upon their sleeves, but take you on a journey of discovery, inviting the eye to follow new avenues and perspectives. Casa del Sabino, his ranch project in Valle de Bravo, is a perfect example, with its many patios, terraces and corridors leading you from one surprise to the next.

'There is always something to discover here, which is so important,' says de Yturbe. 'You enter through a narrow slit in the high walls and discover the strong patio, and then you go inside again and discover something else, then another terrace, and so on …'

The Casa del Sabino is also filled with the echoes of traditional Mexican architecture, interpreted in a new light. Forming part of a ranch, its layout is reminiscent of the old haciendas, yet the high, sanguine walls also suggest the featureless adobe of the *pueblos*. The large courtyard, where horses can be brought to be mounted, recalls the monumental patios of pre-Hispanic Mexican cities.

Water is a vital element. The main patio has a big pool where the horses can drink. Another terrace, bordered by indigo-blue walls on two sides, but also looking out across the trees and gardens, holds a long swimming pool. The pools and the lofty walls make for a constant play of light and reflection throughout the day. 'The shadows here on the walls are very important,' says de Yturbe. 'You can see the time of day from the shadows. They tell a story.'

LEFT The featureless, tall walls surrounding the house and courtyard suggest a hacienda or a large pueblo. The agave garden reinforces connections with Mexico's heritage and rural past, even within this most contemporary environment.
BELOW The raised swimming-pool terrace has a very different feel and a different colour scheme, but the towering walls remain to the sides, framing a view out across the grounds.

LEFT AND ABOVE *In the hallways and reception rooms alike, there is always a vista to enjoy, often formed by perspective. The dining room (above left), with its large open fire, has a terracotta tiled floor and a table by de Yturbe. The walls of the long corridor leading to the bedrooms (above) is covered in a shining plaster, copied from a monastery in Oaxaca.*

Horses come right into the main courtyard to drink and for mounting. The floor mixes sections of ironwork with clay tiles for contrasting textures, while the planting has been kept to a minimum, focusing the eye on the slab of greenery echoed by the treetops rising above the uppermost edges of the redoubtable, chunky walls.

LEFT AND RIGHT *The colonnades of the hacienda, which is on one level set around a central courtyard, create a welcome sense of space and a fluid shift from indoors to out. Vines playing over the arches cast shadows across the walls, as though nature were creeping right into the house, while through the arches there are views across the dusty valley landscape. On a table to one side of the loggia sits a collection of dead snakes, spiders, scorpions and small animals found around the house, which have been confined to old mayonnaise jars and preserved in formaldehyde by the family's three children.*

CASA EL ARANJUEZ

Between them, James and Alexandra Brown have lived in many parts of the world. James grew up in southern California; with an English father and an Austrian mother, Alexandra was brought up in New Delhi. They have made themselves at home in Tangier, Patmos, Paris and Manhattan. Now their home is Casa el Aranjuez – a renovated hacienda including a Dominican chapel and with parts dating back to the sixteenth century – on valley slopes within the Sierra Madre del Sur, with views of Oaxaca and the ruins of the ancient Zapotec city of Monte Albán in the distance.

They moved here with their three children back in 1995, attracted to the house by the country location and the generous proportions of the rooms. They were introduced to the area by James's brother, Matthew, who works with local Zapotec rug weavers producing hand-made pieces designed by contemporary artists. The couple soon began to place their mark on the house, restoring the gardens and designing rugs and furniture for their home – such as the canopied sofa in the living room and their double bed, with a French tapestry hanging on the wall behind.

James recruited a neglected part of the house to serve as his artist's studio. He has been working on a series of paintings inspired by the poems of D H Lawrence, but together with Alexandra he has also founded the Carpe Diem Press, producing limited editions in conjunction with other artists and using local printers in Oaxaca.

'The liberty of time and of living in the middle of nowhere gives you opportunities,' Brown has said. 'Being able to live in a very isolated way and to work without the daily contacts of life in a big city has been very helpful.'

ABOVE To one side of the kitchen the Browns have created a kind of decorative altar, with Mexican pieces and icons and crosses from all over the world.

RIGHT AND FAR RIGHT In the sitting room (right) a dramatic sofa made to the Browns' design, with a French pelmet for a canopy, has one of James's paintings as its backdrop. James designed their four-poster bed (far right, above) with a local ironmonger and it stands in front of a seventeenth-century French tapestry. The dining-room carpet (far right, below) is also James's design.

LEFT AND RIGHT *Casa Reforma is a visually striking amalgamation of old and new, incorporating the old adobe walls that surrounded the site yet constituting the most contemporary of spaces with a mixture of traditional and very modern materials. The garden complements the house, with strong, seamless connections between the two, such as the dining room that opens out to the pool terrace (right). 'We wanted to create a garden but not in the way that most people think of a garden,' says Héctor Velázquez Graham. 'It's not a garden that lives with grass and plants, but with light, sound and reflections.'*

CASA REFORMA

Oaxaca is a city of artists. Rufino Tamayo and Francisco Toledo, two of the most famous names in modern Mexican art, were born there. And here Sergio Hernández, one of the country's finest contemporary painters, also has his base.

Casa Reforma, Hernández's home, was designed by architect Héctor Velázquez Graham in collaboration with Ramón Torres Martinéz and the artist himself. It is a house that juxtaposes the organic qualities of adobe and other natural materials, such as wood and stone, with glass and structural pieces of steel, while also adopting a code of simplicity that yields the most powerful of results.

Located within the historic centre of Oaxaca, the site of the house was already enclosed by old adobe walls that had to be preserved. The architects used the earthy nature of the walls to their advantage by making adobe the key building block of the house, while ordering the space and flow as a dramatic series of terraces and patios, with the most fluid of divisions between outside and in, and strong contrasts between transparency and solidity.

The courtyard garden, with its large, reflective pool, becomes the centre point, with the main rooms of the house filtering off to the sides, while a sliding screen hangs over the patio as a flexible source of shade. 'Sergio Hernández tried to make this house an example of what you could do in a place like Oaxaca within a modern concept of architecture,' says Velázquez Graham. 'Some resisted the house because they thought it would destroy the area like a germ coming into the city. Now it has opened their eyes.'

There is a choice of seating areas in the house, which offer connections to the courtyard outside with folding glass doors that can be left open or closed. A Noguchi lamp hangs over a wicker sofa and armchairs in one room (left), while the other is more enclosed, arranged with a few pieces of Italian furniture (below left). Both rooms thrive on simplicity, with the texture and patina of the materials chosen providing much of the visual beauty.

ABOVE AND LEFT *A simple spiral staircase, with timber plates set into an iron support, leads to an upstairs studio. Many of the rooms in the house are decorated in a minimal style, but the use of so many organic materials, especially timber and adobe, enriches the space and gives it warmth and interest. 'The house was designed for an artist who is unusual and who is a perfectionist,' says Velázquez Graham. 'It doesn't respect a traditional family way of living.'*

ABOVE AND RIGHT *Striking artwork by Sergio Hernández dominates the entrance hall. In parts of the house the walls are covered with 'masilla', a plaster also used on the walls of the convent of Santo Domingo nearby. During the restoration of the convent, Hernández visited it and was impressed by the beauty of the plaster work. He then suggested inviting the artisans who had worked at Santo Domingo to come and work at Casa Reforma.*

RIGHT *A view from the bathroom to the master bedroom, with a mantis on the wall. Like so many of the finest contemporary buildings in Mexico, the house succeeds through collaboration between architect and artist. 'Hernández is a talented artist with a wonderful vision for colours and light,' enthuses Velázquez Graham.*

LAS POZAS

The late Edward James was a visionary. How else to describe an Englishman who could imagine within the remote mountainside jungle lands of San Luis Potosí a surreal playground, an architectural fantasy, a pleasure garden with little practical purpose – a glorious indulgence for a Don Quixote tilting in New Spain.

James inherited a fortune made in mining and timber, allowing him to do much as he pleased. He had an early career as a novelist and poet; later his generous patronage of the arts led to friendships with the great surrealists Salvador Dalí and René Magritte. Surrealist art clicked with the eccentricities of James's own mind and stimulated his imagination.

In the 1940s, while travelling in Mexico, he heard of a place in the jungle where orchids grew in their thousands. Seeking out the flowers, he resolved to have and to hold this wild garden. But in 1962, a severe winter frost wiped out the orchids. Edward James was appalled, but resolved to create another garden of his own and Las Pozas, named after his garden's jungle water pools, was created in the more enduring form of concrete.

James would design his fantasies and have moulds made to realize them, pouring in the concrete that was supported by metal struts. He created not only giant flowers but Wonderland structures such as the House Destined to be a Cinema, the Toadstool Platform, the Princess Ring, the Fleur-de-Lys Bridge and the Temple of the Ducks. These were sculptures and follies, dreams in the forest, and then he brought electricity into the jungle to illuminate his creation at night. Like the ruins of some great forgotten city, Las Pozas sleeps among the trees.

ABOVE, RIGHT AND FAR RIGHT *Since James's death in 1984, there has been a struggle to preserve and protect Las Pozas. The property is now owned by Plutarco 'Kaco' Gastelum, the son of James's manager and foreman of works, who has kept the jungle garden open to the public. But there is a constant battle to prevent nature from* *swallowing up Las Pozas, especially since James neglected to leave any funds for the preservation of his unique wonderland. The pathways and buildings are always in danger of becoming overgrown by vegetation, while the rains threaten to erode the metal rods and supports that are threaded through the concrete structures.*

COAST

In the state of Quintana Roo on the Yucatán peninsula, the Mayans built the city of Tulum by the sea. Dating back to the sixth century, the 'City of Dawn' is perched on a modest bank of cliffs overlooking the beach and the Caribbean Sea and was built to honour the sun. Farther up the coast, along the 'Mayan Riviera', stands Cancún, a very different city built to honour the sea and the sun. Both suggest that an epic coastline has always been part of the natural allure of Mexico.

The collective shore of this country, with its giant limbs and spurs, is longer than any other in Latin America; the noble Yucatán coast offered a natural gateway into Mexico from Cuba and other Spanish Caribbean territories. On his 1518 expedition from Cuba, Juan de Grijalva spotted Tulum and likened it to Seville; Cortés landed first at Cozumel just up the coast and met Gerónimo de Aguilar who had been shipwrecked here years before and guided him into the Mayan world. The Caribbean territories later became natural dancing partners for the Yucatán and other Spanish colonies in the Gulf of Mexico and settlers and slaves brought with them touches and tastes of Afro-Caribbean culture and customs.

Veracruz, the first settlement founded by Cortés, is often described as a Caribbean city, its music, dress and nightlife strongly coloured by Cuba. It became the great docks and doorway to Spain and Europe. 'You still have that feeling of arrival – from Cortés, Maximilian and Carlota, everything came from Veracruz,' Carlos Fuentes has said. 'Veracruz is where I really feel at home. It's the joyful part of Mexico and to sit in the portals of Veracruz having coffee is to have the feeling of being at the gateway to Mexico. It's very thrilling.'

On the coast nature itself is also the thrill. In the Yucatán, as well as the convent route, the Mayan trail and the hacienda experience, you might also follow the beach map, the *cenote* path and the biosphere tour. The *cenotes*, or sinkholes, follow a curving fracture, supposedly marking the edge of a crater rim made by the meteor that wiped out the dinosaurs. At the biospheres and national parks, you can see flamingo colonies, crocodiles and green iguanas; some say the coral-reef reserve off the Mayan Riviera is second only to Australia's Great Barrier Reef.

On the Pacific coast, too, nature provides a far superior attraction to the great resort towns such as Acapulco. Grey whales cruise the Pacific shores of Baja, while the Gulf of California is a fine place to see blue whales and bottlenose or white-sided dolphins. Along the southern beaches of Jalisco, sea turtles come and lay their eggs year after year, while the deciduous forests are alive with countless species of plants, birds and mammals, and in some sheltered places there are still jaguars and pumas.

PREVIOUS PAGES (LEFT) *An idyllic coastal scene just off the coast road running from Puerto Vallarta southwards to Careyes in the state of Jalisco.* (RIGHT) *The home of Michael Possenbacher in Careyes itself (see page 100) with a view of the terrace and infinity pool.* LEFT *The palapa at the Possenbacher house in Careyes; the palapa allows the creation of 'a terrace with a hat' that is perfect for a Pacific setting like Careyes and becomes the focal point of the house.* ABOVE *Scenes from the Pacific: an iguana soaks up the sun; breaking waves on the beach at Hotelito Desconocido (see page 94); and a man on horseback.*

Here, south of Puerto Vallarta, at Costa Careyes, or the Turtle Coast, Italian designer and entrepreneur Gian Franco Brignone founded an idyllic enclave of houses and retreats overlooking the Pacific. Brignone first spotted this stretch of coastline on a plane trip in 1968 and he began the gradual process of creating a haven for the blessed there, a private multi-cultural community where development is carefully governed and the houses designed in sympathy with the environment.

Brignone designed a number of houses at Careyes himself; today his home is a hilltop hideaway called Tigre del Mar, a modern-day fortress on the cliffs painted in blue, with spectacular views out across the ocean – and Careyes itself – from the horizon room at the summit of the tallest tower. Here Brignone has let his imagination run freely, experimenting with bold colours; organic, sculpted shapes; and unusual materials, such as titanium mixed with concrete for the sinuous stairway climbing up the centre of Tigre del Mar. A series of five terraces maximize the stunning views and the relationship with life outdoors, while steps carved into the cliffs reach down to a subterranean grotto.

Other architects and designers have made their mark upon the houses of Careyes: Manolo Mestre, Duccio Ermenegildo and Alex Possenbacher. The latter now lives and works in Careyes, having been invited by his father Michael to help him build a house on a slice of clifftop in the early 1990s. The house was the first of a number of Possenbacher's projects to play with the vernacular style of the *palapa* within a contemporary, highly comfortable environment. 'The *palapa* is not so much a room as a terrace with a hat that creates a very informal living room,' says Possenbacher. 'It's on this coast that it really began to be popular in modern architecture. It's an easy way to make a light, large-scale structure and it's also very thermic, allowing the room to breathe. But it's also flexible so it's good in earthquakes and good in the wind, because each layer of palm leaves works like a vent.'

The architect and his architect wife, Lorena, have now built their own *palapa* house at Careyes. But back in the early 1990s, it was all much harder; the road to Careyes was little more than a track and there were no telephones. Constructing Casa Cayman for Michael Possenbacher took two and a half years.

Alix Marcaccini and her family started visiting Careyes in the mid-1980s. 'It was much wilder then and the natural environment even more powerful than it is now', she says. 'One really felt at the end of the world and nature was stronger than everything. There were no telephones, no television. It was a dream. Modernization has simplified people's lives here but it has also taken away some of its charm.'

Alix's father, Sir James Goldsmith, bought the neighbouring estate of Cuixmala, just along the shore from Careyes, in 1987. This is an extraordinary place, with palm plantations and deciduous forest stretching in all directions. Sir James worked with the designer and architect Robert Couturier to produce La Loma, a breathtaking Indian-inspired palace beside the sea, decorated in cooling white and enlivened with brightly coloured, embroidered fabrics. A magnificent series of steps leads you down to the beachhead, where there is a swimming pool and a *palapa* pool house.

'My father was looking for a place where he could be totally self-contained and self-sufficient with food and water,' says Alix Marcaccini. 'He loved being here because of the beauty of the place but also because everything was so pure with organically grown food and the fresh air. He involved himself in every aspect of running the estate.'

Cuixmala is now managed by Alix and her husband Goffredo Marcaccini, who live for much of the year in their own house on the estate with their three daughters. It is a demanding role, given that the estate covers nearly 370 hectares (3,000 acres) and includes organic farming and organizing the rental of a number of idyllic houses and *casitas* on the estate, including La Loma itself. There is also the task of overseeing the Cuixmala Ecological Foundation, which Sir James set up to try to protect the forest habitat around Cuixmala.

'When my father-in-law understood the importance of these deciduous and semi-deciduous forests, which are unique to Jalisco and the lowland Pacific Coast, he started buying up land behind Cuixmala with the objective of protecting them,' says Goffredo Marcaccini. 'He bought around 25,000 acres and set up the Foundation. Compared to the time when the Spaniards

arrived, when the forest was in pristine condition, we have only two per cent of the forest left. Projecting into the future, in 25 years the only dry deciduous and semi-deciduous forest that will survive in Jalisco may be in the Chamela-Cuixmala Biosphere Reserve.'

The secure reserve is jointly sponsored by the Foundation and the National University of Mexico. There have been programmes to conserve the sea turtles which lay their eggs along Cuixmala's two and a half miles of beach, and projects to conserve crocodiles, parrots, jaguars and pumas. In the reserve, says Goffredo, there are 1,200 species of vascular plants, 270 species of birds, 72 of mammals, 68 of reptiles and 19 of amphibians, making this neo-tropical region one of the greatest areas of biodiversity in the world.

Along this coastline there are other retreats, such as Hotelito Desconocido and Verana, which also adopt eco-consciousness as part of their philosophy, pushing back the tyrannies of modern living as though the beauty of this environment demands it. Marcello Murzilli, the owner and founder of Hotelito, and another Italian, was also enchanted by the natural power of this coastal world. Having sold his fashion empire and then spent two years sailing around the world, he had come to appreciate the value, strength and fragility of the natural environment. When he came across the lagoon location of Hotelito, Murzilli decided to adopt an ecologically aware approach using local materials, with no electricity and no distractions. The result is one of the most romantic and pleasurable of escapes, especially at night when everything is lit by candlelight and flares.

'I was lucky to believe in the idea and to prove that you can mix luxury with vernacular architecture,' says Murzilli. 'You are within a nature reserve at Hotelito, so the construction had to be very natural and we really believed that electricity was not necessary. From the first day I thought we should really create something more ecologically friendly. The mix of nature, ecology and glamour produced something quite unique.'

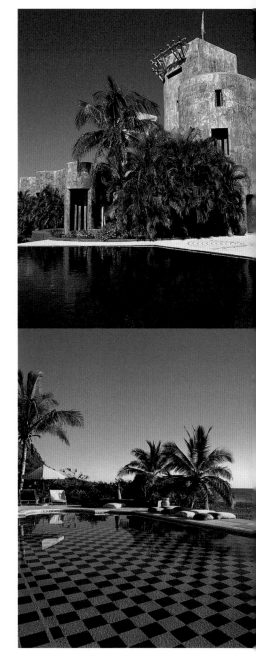

ABOVE *Brignone's house at Careyes, set on a clifftop above the Pacific coast and overlooking the village he created. Beneath is the beach pool at La Loma, built by Sir James Goldsmith at his Cuixmala estate.*

HOTELITO DESCONOCIDO

LEFT *Right on the edge of the lagoon, a palafito offers perfect views of the birdlife and the sunset over the Pacific. With its stilted design, thatched roof and terrace, complete with a hammock, the palafito echoes traditional Pacific coastal architecture, not just of Mexico but also of Hawaii and Polynesia. The use of natural materials and colours means that the exterior of the building blends with the landscape, rather than fighting against it.*

RIGHT *The interiors of the palafitos mix simplicity and sophistication in equal measure. As can be seen here in El Melon, each room has an individual theme loosely inspired by its name, which generates the motifs and gently influences the colours and style of the interior. The adobe walls and wood floor and ceiling supports are decorated in colours that are familiar Mexican pigments.*

Like so many of the very best Mexican hotels, the Hotelito Desconocido lies at the end of a long dirt track. The turning from the coast road, running south of Puerto Vallarta towards Manzanillo, takes you to the dusty village of Cruz de Loreto and then on towards the sea, past fields of figs and avocado. As you turn through the wooden gates of Hotelito, there is little suggestion of the enchantment to come.

Set around a lagoon where the pelicans fish, Hotelito is the very personal creation of Marcello Murzilli. He was travelling along the coast of Jalisco when he stumbled across what would one day become Hotelito, arranged on either side of the estuary with a small fleet of rowing boats carrying you between the two.

'I found this beautiful natural reserve, and I told the local villagers that I wanted to do something and said if you help me we can try,' says Murzilli. 'So the story began. I lived in a tent here for three years while the place was built with the help of 150 local people – the same people who work at Hotelito now. It was a strange, beautiful adventure because it's hand-made and because everything was done with a lot of passion.'

A fashion designer turned hotelier, Murzilli planned the *palafitos*, or stilted huts, around the lagoon in adobe, timber, bamboo and thatch. He was inspired by traditional Mexican architecture, especially the stilted houses built by the coast around Veracruz. With these individually decorated *palafitos*, a restaurant and bar projecting over the waters of the lagoon and across on the other side, the beach and sea pool with its *palapa* lounge, this is the most enticing of escapes.

ABOVE AND RIGHT *In houses built of mud and bamboo, Murzilli has created the most romantic and tranquil of retreats. The mix of simplicity and a sophisticated eye distinguishes palafito bedrooms (above, top left and below right), the reception area with a dramatic chandelier hanging overhead (above, below left) and the bar and restaurant (above, top right), which cantilevers out over the lagoon. A charming collection of Mexican miracle paintings and a miniature shrine decorate one end of the bar (right).*

ABOVE *The restaurant and bar, El Cantarito, seen from the seaward side of the lagoon and illuminated by candlelight at dusk. The tower has a dining table for a romantic and personal meal — always a favourite of honeymooners. The pool is on the beach, named Nopalito.*

LEFT *From the summit of the tower diners can gaze across the lagoon to Nopalito and the beach stretching out along the coast. The beach is a magnet for turtles who come to lay their eggs here year after year, under the protective eye of the Hotelito staff.*

BELOW *This palafito's shower enjoys a view of the lagoon – and pelicans diving for their breakfast.*

CASA CAYMAN

Antiques dealer Michael Possenbacher arrived in Mexico from Germany in the 1950s and has lived here ever since. He made his home in Mexico City for many years, but after the earthquake of 1985 he began looking for a more peaceful part of the country for himself and his wife. Careyes was the place they eventually fell in love with.

Working in collaboration with his son, architect Alex Possenbacher, he came up with an inspirational design for Casa Cayman that maximized both the potential of the setting and the breathtaking views out across the Pacific Ocean. The heart of the house is the *palapa* living room, moving seamlessly out towards the open terraces of the house and the infinity pool, reaching into the sea.

The *palapa* with its timber supports enclosed in vine wood and a vast stag fern tumbling down, the floors made with stone from the Yucatán, the sculpted rattan chairs, the vaulted and curving ceilings of the bedroom wing, the soft and warm earthy colours: together all these create the impression of the most organic of homes. 'And the garden in Careyes is the ocean,' says Michael Possenbacher. 'Instead of a park, you have the sea.'

A collection of contemporary artwork, antiques and sculptures has also formed part of the design of the house, including integrated pieces such as the eighth-century Indian columns by the pool, while the mascot of the house is the vintage Mexican cayman, or crocodile, mask in the master bedroom. A soothing, sociable house where nature meets nurture, and simplicity is part of its sophistication, Casa Cayman is at the heart of Careyes.

LEFT Many antiques and geological treasures have been woven into the design of the house. The granite columns by the pool, for instance (below left), are eighth-century Indian. The round canonball-like pieces in the stone basin are Mexican 'bombas del volcano' (below right). The rounded wicker chairs underneath the palapa were designed by Michael Possenbacher (above right), and the pillars that support the palapa are made of a local wood, as hard as ebony at its centre, covered in vine growth. 'It looks like Art Nouveau,' observes Possenbacher.

ABOVE In the dining area located on a raised level overlooking the main terrace, an ammonite has been skilfully incorporated into the wall. The colours are soothing and fit well with the natural tones of the stone and wood used throughout the house.

ABOVE RIGHT In the master bedroom an alligator (part of a dancer's costume) lies on a dividing wall, acting as the house's cayman mascot; the table in front of the wall is seventeenth-century Mexican.

RIGHT A covered terrace is comfortably furnished and provides a cool refuge from the heat of the sun.

LEFT, BELOW LEFT AND BELOW *In the large lounge bedroom, the painting above the fireplace is by Francisco Toledo (left) while the little chair is Mexican. On a polychrome Mexican eighteenth-century table rests a pair of ornate Mexican cruciform stirrups from the colonial era, with another Toledo on the wall behind (below left). Michael Possenbacher designed the mast-like lampshades, using fifteenth-century Asian vases as bases (below). The chest is Dutch, from the sixteenth century. All this suggests the home of a serious collector with a wide-ranging interest in art and antiques.*

ABOVE *The chest is Mexican, in embroidered leather, while the relief is Italian Renaissance. The curving form of the room's design gives a cool, cavernous feel to the room. 'The house looks very organic,' says Alex Possenbacher, 'but actually it's also very mathematical.'*

LEFT AND RIGHT 'It was a
blank canvas,' says Manolo
Mestre. 'It was a beautiful
clifftop site but with little
land to build on, so we
spent a whole year taming
the land. We had this 180-
degree view, and although
it's one house I wanted
to create the feeling of
multiple spaces and views.
So, for instance, you can
have your lunch looking
across to the island or
dinner looking down at
the beach in the distance.'

CASA LUNA

'Everything I have done in Careyes is an explosion of colour,' says Manolo Mestre. 'Colour belongs to Careyes and it's one of my favourite places because there is such a sense of unity.'

The architect and designer has now applied his skills to a handful of houses in Careyes – all of them designed around a *palapa*. Casa Luna is one of those designed by Mestre, a family home for the Tribull family, who spend part of the year here and part of it working and living in Los Angeles. The site offered a blank canvas, facing the sea, and the design of the house caresses the hillside, while juxtaposing purposefully natural elements such as the *palapa* and man-made materials such as the polished or chiselled cement floors.

'I like to work with highly contemporary, clean surfaces and the baroqueness of natural textures,' says Mestre. 'And with a *palapa* I always aim to invent a new vocabulary and a new design with every one that I do, just like weaving a spider's web. And one of the unique things about the *palapa* is that it creates this cathedral-like structure that allows the house to breathe.'

Drawing upon a wealth of Mexican architectural influences, Mestre explored every detail of the house and its interiors, designing furniture that was made by local artisans, and emphasizing the tactile qualities of the space. A monolithic fountain at the entrance of the house was inspired by the baptismal fonts of the old convents; the bird-of-paradise motif in the floor of the main courtyard, ringed by palms, recalls an Aztec symbol.

LEFT The painting of an undersea world in the palapa sitting room was done by Sergio Hernández, especially for the house. All of the furniture was designed by Mestre and the side lamps were made locally.

RIGHT The patterns in the floors of Casa Luna have particular significance. At the entrance there is the moon, which is the emblem of the house, then the font-like fountain within a circle with circular motifs on the floor, while in the courtyard, surrounded by palm trees, a bird of paradise is set into the centre, a replica of an Aztec symbol (right centre). The use of stone and chiselled or polished cement floors provides different textures through the house. 'In a house like this you are always barefoot, so it's good to bring in a tactile element,' says Mestre. 'I believe in tactile architecture.'

ABOVE Within the house the bold use of colour is striking, sun tones in oranges and reds predominating. The pots and planters were all chosen in consultation with the owners. 'I like to take my clients to arts and crafts studios to see where their furniture and ceramics are made,' says Mestre. 'In this case we went to a village in Oaxaca where they made the pots. Every single object in this house has a history.'

LEFT AND BELOW LEFT
The beds are designed as built-in platforms, emerging from the floor.

BELOW The bathrooms also have a sculpted, cohesive quality, while man-made materials such as the concrete floors contrast with the use of natural elements such as the palapa. 'I like to juxtapose natural and modern materials,' says Mestre, 'and explore highly contemporary, clean surfaces.'

LEFT *The sitting room, with its vaulted brickwork ceilings and polished cement floors, holds an eclectic collection of furniture and textiles. On the wall behind the couch are lengths of decorated tapa cloth from Fiji, made of thin pieces of barkwood, which would have been used as skirts for the head of a tribe, while the draped fabrics on the equipale chairs are from Indonesia. The furniture in the house is partly Mexican, mixed with some from North Africa, although many pieces, such as the sofa, have been built into the fabric of the house.*

RIGHT *One of the main bedrooms at Casa Arcadia, again with dramatic vaulted ceilings. This is a house that steadily, subtly evolves over the years. The Marcaccinis have three daughters, two of whom were born at Cuixmala, so the building has grown upwards to hold more bedrooms. An additional guest bedroom has been added on to the top of the house, on a roof terrace, while the terrace itself was pushed up a level.*

CASA ARCADIA

From the home of Alix and Goffredo Marcaccini, the view is one of palm trees and forest canopy stretching out towards the sea and the domed outline of La Loma, the Indian-inspired palace that her father built on the ocean edge. It is a sublime location, wrapped in nature, and is the family home that the couple share with their three daughters, two of whom were born here at Cuixmala.

Casa Arcadia was one of the few houses that already existed at Cuixmala when Sir James Goldsmith bought the estate in the 1980s. Alix worked closely with her father on remodelling the house, deciding on all the details. Casa Arcadia, with its patios, large veranda, pool and gardens, has been evolving ever since, having recently been extended to incorporate a new guest room and roof terrace. 'We wanted an open, simple feel for the house, as well as comfort,' says Alix. 'I love the earth tones and the view, which is a dream.'

The interiors are given an added sense of drama and generosity of proportion by the vaulted brickwork ceilings – a traditional Mexican element with a Moorish flavour. The shining white of the polished cement floors and the light, natural colours of the walls offer a clean backdrop to an eclectic mix of textiles and artwork that have been gathered by the Marcaccinis from Africa, Guatemala and Indonesia, as well as Mexico itself.

'My father-in-law wanted to create a place where you could be surrounded by beauty in comfort and privacy, breathing fresh air, eating healthily,' says Goffredo of Cuixmala. At Casa Arcadia the Marcaccinis continue the philosophy.

ABOVE AND LEFT *The soft, earthy tones of the house generate a warm, relaxed atmosphere. The organic neutrality provides a perfect backdrop for antique pieces such as the religious icon in the hallway (above) or twentieth-century classics such as the Le Corbusier recliner (left). 'It's more Careyes style than traditionally Mexican,' says Alix Marcaccini. 'But perhaps it's a little simpler than some of the houses in Careyes.'*

Casa Vigil

The feeling at Casa Vigil is one of serenity and calm. This is a Careyes *palapa* home, but with a very contemporary – almost minimal – attitude, which only heightens the sense of escape from the pressures of everyday life. Soothing colours, earth tones and a minimum of distractions lead you naturally out under the *palapa* and towards the curving pool and terraces facing the sea, dotted with hump-backed islands.

Designer Margarita Alvarez was first commissioned to work on the house in the mid-1980s, but was recently asked to remodel and update the house using a softer palette of colours, while still retaining the organic feel of the spaces. 'It's always very important to me to work with natural materials, especially in projects that are themselves surrounded by nature', says Alvarez, who has worked across Mexico and the United States, 'and integrating ethnic art, especially Mexican, is always a key objective'.

The simple, sculpted quality of Casa Vigil is enhanced by the many pieces of integrated furniture, which seem to emerge, like moulded clay, from the floor, including beds and sofas scattered with cushions in gentle, muted colours. The inlaid mosaic floor at the heart of the sitting room was inspired by a sixteenth-century design, made with locally sourced black and white stones, while an iron sculpture in the sitting room was suggested by a Mayan design and is named 'Xooc', or 'Radiance'. This is a place where every detail has been considered and the house, set amid water and vibrant greenery, is perfectly attuned to its environment.

LEFT The main living area beneath the palapa features a large built-in sofa with an iron sculpture behind it inspired by a Mayan design. Inlaid into the floor is a square stone 'rug', made of black and white round stones found locally. Nearby are some contemporary iron lamps, designed by Alvarez.

BELOW The yellow tones of the semi-circular wall in the guest bedroom stand out against the neutral whites. The wall, with its porthole, serves as headboard and room divider separating off the entrance area.

LEFT AND ABOVE *A child's bedroom, featuring one of Alvarez's sculpted beds that became part of the fabric of the room (left); a trough filled with onyx stones on one side of the guest bedroom's circular wall (above); and part of the hallway to the master bedroom with five terracotta pots modelled on olive-oil jars (above).*

REVIVAL

The Mexican Revolution has been described as a sweeping away of the past, erasing the haciendas and *hacendados* (hacienda owners), the pretensions of Neo-classical architecture, ostentatious European fashions and tastes, and a mass of inequality and injustice. It was, in fact, a complicated and disorderly affair, with ten years of instability, war and chaos only ending in the early 1920s. It was the most painful of births for modern Mexico.

After the Revolution, Mexico was slowly rebuilt in countless ways. For the next 30 or 40 years, within a great outpouring of creative thought, Mexican architects and designers sought to create a new identity for their country. Some looked outwards to the example of the pioneering Modernists in the United States and Europe, to Le Corbusier and the Bauhaus leaders; Hannes Meyer, the Swiss head of Bauhaus during the late 1920s, even settled in Mexico in 1939. Others looked more closely around them, re-examining traditional architecture: the *pueblos* and old towns, the monumental Mayan and Aztec structures, and the fusion styles of the early colonial era.

There began a gradual renaissance of Mexican architecture; the past had not been swept away after all but was instead reinvented and reborn, taking inspiration from the roots of Mexico's rich architectural and artisan culture. But at its most interesting, this neo-Mexican design was combined with a Modernist influence. The patios and terraces of the Mayans were reborn in concrete, the great featureless walls of the *pueblos* remade in brick and breeze blocks, the fountains and irrigation pools of the haciendas reinvented in cement.

At the same time Mexican art was going through a similar transformation, the two disciplines re-energizing one another. Most famously Diego Rivera became the standard bearer of Mexico's new culture, expressing his ideas in the vast 1920s murals funded by government grants, enlivening the public buildings and depicting revolutionary, historical and social themes in a palette of vibrant colours and a vivid contemporary style. José Clemente Orozco, Alfaro David Siqueiros and Rivera formed a triumvirate of muralists and artists interested not just in politics and the rise of *mestizo* Mexico, but also in new techniques and ways of expressing themselves.

Some artists crossed over the boundary into architecture. Juan O'Gorman was an architect and painter initially drawn towards Modernism and an international style, but later, like many others, he began to rethink the Mexican vernacular in new contexts and materials. The unusually strong relationship between Mexican art and architecture has filtered down to leading contemporary architects such as Teodoro González de León and Agustín Hernández, who practice as both artist and sculptor, while Ricardo Legorreta has collaborated with the artist Francisco Toledo, as well as being inspired by the bold use of colours in twentieth-century Mexican art.

PREVIOUS PAGES (LEFT) *The spiral staircase of the Art Deco Edificio Bassurto apartment building in Parque España in the Condesa district of Mexico City was designed by Francisco Bassurto.* (RIGHT) *Luis Barragán's Capilla de Tlalpan, Mexico City, which was built in the 1950s, and eventually completed in 1960.*

LEFT *Agustín Hernández's futuristic home and office, perched on a valley hillside in Mexico City and seeming to hover above the ground like a spaceship.*

ABOVE *Diego Rivera's studio, designed by Juan O'Gorman; the Arcos Bosque building by Teodoro González de León; and the factory floor of the Bacardi Factory by Felix Candela, all in Mexico City.*

Luis Barragán, the godfather of modern Mexican design, was an architect, artist and poet. He loved colour and its ability to transform and enliven buildings and spaces. Colour meant the bold, warm, natural pigments remembered from his childhood in Guadalajara, but also the colours of his travels in Spain, Morocco and the Mediterranean. The simplicity and purity of Barragán's self-taught architecture is given a key dimension by colour, whether the dusty pinks of his neo-hacienda, Cuadra San Cristóbal, or the contrasting tones of his sculptural Satellite Towers on the Querétaro Highway in Mexico City, designed with sculptor Mathias Goeritz. His global influence stretched into the movement we now call minimalism, yet contrary to much of that genre's achievements, Barragán's work was never cold or clinical, but was warmed and enriched by his use of colour, shadows and light.

Barragán was born in 1902 in the state of Jalisco. His memories of landscape, villages and towns, churches and even the fountains and watercourses of his childhood ('the dark ponds in the recess of abandoned orchards; the curbstone of shallow wells in the convent patios …') were to have a profound effect on Barragán. Yet he was no isolationist and his ideas about the importance of context, landscape and setting, the serenity and contemplative qualities of a conceived space, did not spring simply from his close observations of Mexican vernacular and colonial architecture.

Barragán was also a traveller. From 1925 to 1927 he undertook an European tour, one of several formative trips. In France he attended lectures by Le Corbusier and weighed the influence of the growing Modernist agenda. In Spain he immersed himself in period architecture and the Islamic influence, beginning to see the architecture of New Spain and its components in a fresh light. Barragán was able to take a wide spectrum of inspirations and influences and fuse them into a unique, clear and powerful vision.

Settling in Mexico in 1936, he began an extraordinary career during which a modest number of his projects would have a global impact. Modernism was spliced with traditionalism, but the combination was seamless. His buildings were geometric, simple and sculptural but also poetic, natural, serene. Much of Barragán's work was residential, but he devoted considerable attention to landscaping, creating a strong relationship between house and land, and using soft, seductive elements, especially water pools and fountains, to calm and caress the whole.

Later, landscape design grew even more important. At his 106-hectare (865-acre) El Pedregal development outside Mexico City, housing design was almost secondary to the importance of the gardens. 'In the creation of a garden,' he said, 'the architect invites the partnership of the kingdom of nature. In a beautiful garden the majesty of nature is ever present, but nature reduced to human proportions and thus transformed into the most efficient haven against the aggressiveness of contemporary life.'

Partly because of Barragán's respect for nature and its colours, his work offered the most beautiful and acceptable face of Modernism and made him the figurehead architect

of Mexico. He helped to make its landscape and its past a part of his vision, while also creating something fresh and enticing. Perhaps what is most striking about his work is that it feels as original today as it did in the middle decades of the twentieth century; he died in 1988.

Ricardo Legorreta, who is perhaps Mexico's most influential and widely recognized contemporary architect, draws his inspiration from many of the same sources as Barragán: old ranches, towns and villages as well as the architecture of Spain. The influence of pre-Hispanic architecture can also be seen within the ziggurat design of parts of the landmark Hotel Camino Royal in Mexico City, which is one of the first large-scale projects by the practice of Legorreta & Legorreta.

'Our work is very much influenced by Mexican culture,' says Ricardo Legorreta. 'We're influenced by pre-Hispanic architecture in the sense of space and of an almost spartan architecture. And in Mexico we have the combination of the two cultures – Hispanic and Indian – which had led to a very special sense of scale. So we are used to ample spaces. But it's also really important to us that each project relates to its location and has a very definite respect for its environment.'

Unlike Barragán, whose work was concentrated across Mexico City, Legorreta's commissions have taken him around Mexico and beyond to the United States and even Europe. The Metropolitan Cathedral in Managua, Nicaragua, with a striking sequence of small domes, was an accomplished step forward in his portfolio of public projects, such as the Main Library in San Antonio, Texas, and the Museum of Fashion and Textiles in London.

Similarly, the work of Teodoro González de León has stretched far beyond the borders of Mexico. His work on the Mexican embassies in Berlin, Belize, Guatemala and Brazil represents the public face of contemporary Mexican architecture. In Mexico City his work is highly visible in the form of monumental, geometric landmark buildings such as the towering Los Arcos, a squared-off-horseshoe office building, and the Federal Law Courts. Impressed by pre-Hispanic and colonial architecture, González de León was also influenced by Le Corbusier and Mies van der Rohe, creating a style that ties Mexican elements closely to international Modernism.

Much of the experimentation and shifts in style have come through the evolving structural possibilities of the building materials themselves. Felix Candela, born in Spain but making Mexico his home from 1939 until his death in 1997, pioneered the use of arching concrete shells to construct dramatic vaulted churches, warehouses and public buildings such as the Olympic Stadium in Mexico City. Agustín Hernández, too, has pushed the structural boundaries of concrete, creating futuristic towering houses in the air, propped up by steel supports sinking deep into the ground. He was heavily influenced by Mayan and other monumental Indian architecture yet has taken this inspiration and pushed it in quick, unexpected directions. He is one of many Mexican architects who, in the modern era, flourished in a climate of innovation and invention.

ABOVE *Work by Ricardo Legorreta: a private house in Mexico City; the entrance area of the Camino Real Hotel in Mexico City; and a bar off the main lobby of the Camino Real Hotel. The latter was finished in 1968, one of his most famous and widely seen projects. 'It was important in the development of my philosophy,' says Legorreta, 'and was the first large-scale project that I had done. To design an absolutely contemporary hotel at a time when the prevailing mood in hotels was bad taste was very important to me.'*

LEFT AND RIGHT The Capilla de Tlalpan, which was completed in 1960, is perhaps the most mesmeric and photogenic of Luis Barragán's projects, mainly because of the masterful use and shaping of light and colour within this relatively simple building. Working with artists Mathias Goeritz and Jesús Reyes, Barragán used amber glass in the windows of the chapel to cast these extraordinary tones around the space, as well as rich, reflective gold leaf on the triptych panels surrounding the altar and a deep, vibrant orange for the textured walls. The effect is one of being bathed in colour and light.

CAPILLA DE TLALPAN

'Being a Catholic I have frequently visited with reverence the now-empty monumental monastic buildings that we inherited from ... our colonial ancestors,' said Luis Barragán. 'I have always been deeply moved by the peace and well-being to be experienced when visiting those uninhabited cloisters and solitary courts. How I have wished that these feelings may leave their own mark in my work.'

And, of course, they did. Nowhere more so than at the Capilla de Tlalpan, or Capuchinas Chapel, in Mexico City. Barragán's chapel is a hymn of light, colour and beauty, despite being built with the simplest of ingredients such as concrete, timber and plaster. Given the limited budget available, Barragán subsidized the costs himself and created a building that seems to capture and distil daylight to imbue the most atmospheric and serene of moods; indeed, the achievement of serenity in a building was one of Barragán's perpetual ambitions.

One of his greatest and most alluring successes was his Cuadra San Cristóbal stud farm at Los Clubes, a combination of house, stables, water pools and gardens. Here nature and architecture seem to exist hand in hand, an impression heightened by the seductive power of the water and fountains. The geometric lines of Cuadra San Cristóbal are warmed by the use of shades of pink and red for the monumental walls, while the open and generous scale of the farm recalls the old Mexican haciendas. Here Barragán proved that modernity and the past, the natural and the man-made, really could live together in absolute harmony.

ABOVE *A studio in the Gálvez House in San Angel, Mexico City, finished in 1955. The painting of a nude with lilies on the facing wall is by Diego Rivera; the folding screen in the foreground introduces a burst of colour in an otherwise predominantly neutral space.*

ABOVE *The mathematical neatness of this display wall at the Gálvez House, coated in an eye-catching pink, echoes the design of the house itself with its regular, geometrical modernism softened by colour and the gently landscaped gardens.*

ABOVE AND RIGHT *Luis Barragán said, 'A fountain brings us peace, joy and restful sensuality.' At Cuadra San Cristóbal, Los Clubes, Mexico City, nature and architecture co-exist, with the colours of the walls acting as a bridge between the two, softening the artificiality of the buildings.*

BELOW Arguably Barragán's
most famous project, and
created in collaboration with
Andrés Casillas, Cuadra San
Cristóbal is still a working
horse ranch, while the
stables, horse pools and
courtyards invoke memories
of haciendas. Barragán was
a horseman himself and
kept a horse at Los Clubes,
on the outskirts of the
capital, for many years.

LEFT AND RIGHT 'When you come into a courtyard, then you feel at peace,' says Ricardo Legorreta. 'In our contemporary world we need this peace of mind.' The courtyard at his house was designed in close collaboration with the artist Francisco Toledo, who he admires because 'Toledo always creates incredible surprises.' To the right we see the courtyard from Legorreta's desk; there are a number of desks and places to work and write scattered around the house. In a corner of the bedroom, light filters in through wooden shutters made of a tropical hardwood from southern Mexico with an intense colour (left). The same wood has been used for the floors.

CASA LEGORRETA

Most of the large family houses in the Lomas district of Mexico, a residential area developed in the 1930s and 1940s, are laid out on traditional lines – every room has its own separate and distinct function. When Ricardo Legorreta came to build his own house he wanted to create something different, something more contemporary that still reflected his love of colour, texture and form gleaned from his passion for traditional Mexican and Moorish architecture.

'I wanted to have a feeling of amplitude rather than having many rooms,' says Legorreta, 'and I wanted to create a very informal way of living. I'm not a formal person. And throughout the house I wanted to bring in light and colour and make it easy and very romantic.'

The open-plan arrangement of the house yielded a handful of spaces: the entrance area, including the garage with cars stacked one above the other; the main living area; the bedroom/library; and the bathroom with its own exercise pool. Lastly there is the courtyard, designed in collaboration with artist Francisco Toledo. 'The courtyard is another tradition we inherited from the Islamic world and it works very well in a place like Mexico City because it isolates you from the stress of the street and the rush of the world.'

Suffused with vibrant colour and rich with light, Casa Legorreta is representative of the best of Legorreta's individual approach. It is distinguished, like so much of his design work, around a generosity of scale and a deep understanding of the dynamics of space and volume.

LEFT The bedroom (top left), and three views of the general living space. 'My first idea was to maintain a Mexican way of living, but also to address a fresh, contemporary style,' says Legorreta. 'So I wanted less individual spaces – in the end it's really four. There's the space in which I live, eat and work. There's the entrance area, including the garage (I like cars). The third is the bedroom, with storage for clothes and books, my main source of inspiration. Then there is the bathroom.' Colour throughout the house is reserved to highlight walls, alcoves and corners.

ABOVE, ABOVE RIGHT AND RIGHT The stairway, courtyard and bathroom, which includes an exercise pool. Everywhere, Legorreta stresses the importance of scale and proportion, light and colour. 'I would say that it's representative of my work, but perhaps unusual in the sense that there is this small number of spaces. But throughout, in all of them, I wanted to bring in light and colour and make it very easy and romantic. I am a romantic, absolutely.'

LEFT AND RIGHT *Agustín Hernández is a sculptor and artist, as well as an architect. His futuristic houses have a sculpted, surreal quality, including the Casa en el Aire, which projects 18 metres (60 feet) from a hillside in the Lomas district of Mexico City. The entrance and car port are at the top of the house, by a roadway, while patios and a pool have been constructed at the foot of the tower. A set of monumental, Mayan-like steps ascends the hill to one side of the terrace, forming an ordered, stately series of small terraces.*

Casa en el Aire

'I tried to be different,' says Agustín Hernández. 'I tried to look for a real Mexican architecture, to look for a way to revisit the pre-Hispanic roots of our history – not only forms but symbolism – to create a synthesis of influences. It was about looking for identity.'

The extraordinary architecture of Agustín Hernández, then, takes imagery and inspiration from the days of the Mayans and the Aztecs; a current fascination happens to be a series of Mayan archaeological museums that he is designing in Mexico and Guatemala. Yet his work looks distinctly twenty-first century, owing much to innovations in the structural use of materials and the inspiration of science fiction. Hernández brings together the past and the future to concoct the most dramatic of presents.

A sculptor and symbolist, a geometrist and engineer, Hernández makes houses that do feel like machines for living in, while his public projects, such as the triptych of tilted crosses that forms his striking Ecumenical Chapel at Mexico City's Military College, are grand experiments in space and form.

The Casa en el Aire is typical of his belief that architecture should strive towards the status of art. The house was designed and built in concrete and steel for a cousin who offered Hernández *carte blanche*; all was created within one clear and individual concept. 'I like it,' the architect says, 'because it's an example of what I strive for in architecture, which is that structure, form and function have to come together as a whole, like nature. It's about unity.'

LEFT AND RIGHT *As well as a sculpture, the house is a complex geometrical puzzle. The complexities of the rather mathematical form of the exterior come into the inside in the angular, yet ordered, layout of many of the rooms in this Bond-like lair. Materials are a mix of the highly man-made – steel, concrete and glass – with more organic elements such as wood and stone. 'The idea', says Hernández, 'was to create a machine house in the air.'*

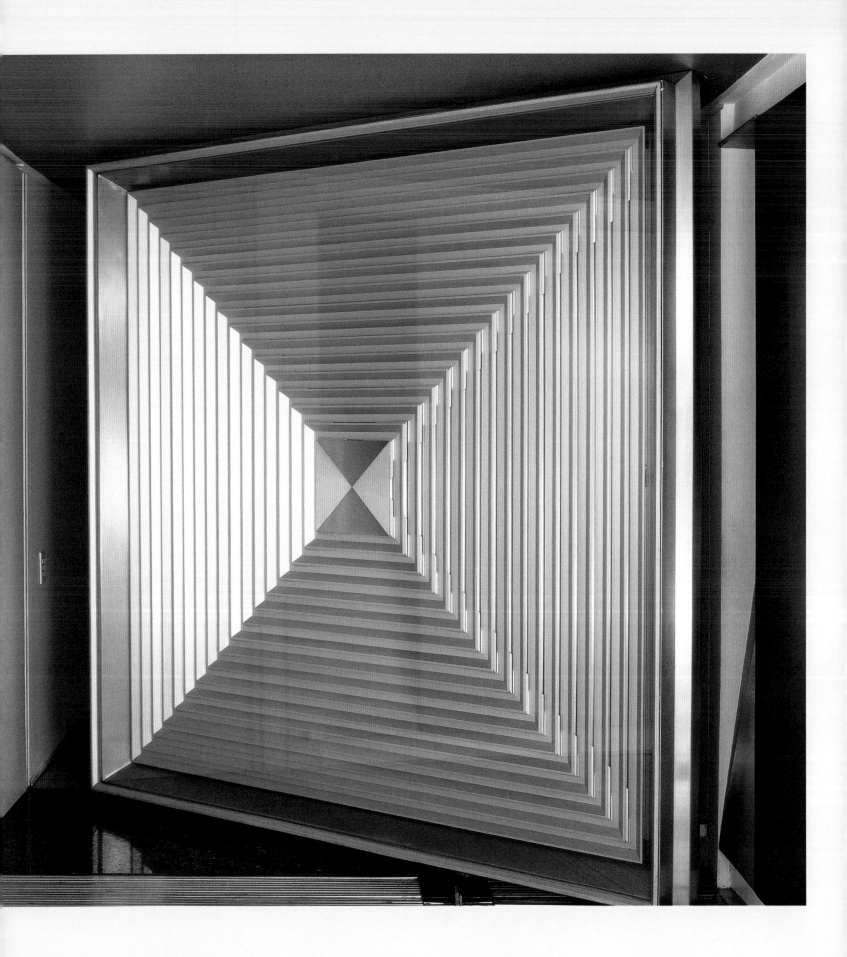

Hernández's approach is to design a house in its entirety. This includes structural elements such as the dramatic stairway and vast electric, pivoting, steel entrance door (far left), but also the furniture, which results in a cohesive space within a highly individual vision. 'When you create a singular, special space, the architecture has a language,' explains Hernández, 'so it's very important that the furniture integrates properly with the architecture.'

CASA AMSTERDAM

The heart of Casa Amsterdam, Teodoro González de León's Mexico City home, is surely the vast studio at the back of the house. It feels like a laboratory, being filled with books and work tables where the architect conceives his artwork, many pieces of which inhabit the house itself. His collages and paintings are typically peopled with geometrical flourishes and intersecting shapes. Some look like building models taken to their most abstract and experimental, some are reminiscent of Casa Amsterdam.

The architecture of González de León is all about intersection and intervention. Los Arcos is a monolithic slab with a void at its centre; his Fonda de Cultura Económica in Mexico City is essentially an irregular semi-circular structure pierced at its apex by a great triangular sword of steel.

Casa Amsterdam offers a contrast to the monumental city architecture that has earned González de León international respect, but still has the same sense of play with form, perspective and line. 'It's a collage of different forms on one level,' he says. 'But essentially it follows a horseshoe pattern that was invented for houses in Mexico City in the nineteenth century. It's a good plan because it can be adapted to any plot of land to fit its orientation.'

At the centre of the horseshoe lie a patio, a pool and a simple garden with a single palm tree. Here, as elsewhere, natural and man-made elements are juxtaposed: water and concrete, glass and stone. 'It has been said that a house is like an autobiography,' says González de León. 'It's a good sentence and perhaps it's true because I live very well in this house.'

LEFT *A view from the studio into the central courtyard, with its raised bank of turf on a slope and pool to one side. The water helps to cast reflections around this house of white and stone. 'The studio and library are an important part of the house,' says González de León, 'because you have a lot of space, but whichever part of the house you are in you have these long views.'*

RIGHT *The main sitting room with a vaulted opening in the wall to the studio beyond. This small mezzanine level, with a series of high, folding vents, allows light and sound — especially music — to pass between the two rooms and provides a sense of connection in a house that is largely open and fluid, with a close relationship between most of the living spaces and the courtyard.*

LEFT *The courtyard, around which the C-shaped house pivots. The steps lead up towards the master bedroom and the front, streetward side of the house.*

RIGHT *The one splash of colour in the house is reserved for the front door, shown centre left, with its combination of blue and red. This creates a false expectation of what is to come: 'You can put elements of colour in a house, like a doorway or hall, but not the main living spaces where you spend many hours, because for me it interferes with objects, paintings and life,' says González de León. The sitting room (below left and centre), the bedroom (above left) and the studio/ library (below right), with a view of the mezzanine (top right), are painted a calm, neutral white.*

MODERN

Mexico City feels like a country all in itself. A sprawling, epic city and an enigmatic, fascinating, chaotic, confusing, beautiful and intriguing place, it has its own character, pace and conventions that somehow set it apart from the rest of Mexico. As you fly into the city, it seems to go on for ever, stretching away into a horizon bordered by mountains and hills. Within the cityscape, at ground level it appears endless, thrusting out in every direction: a great confederation of neighbourhoods that endows the capital with many faces, hearts and limbs.

The city has become so vast that its inhabitants are creating a new living structure, looking to exist, work and socialize within their local districts and thereby reduce the difficulties of commuting. This trend is gradually turning Mexico City into a collection of interconnected towns. Within the whole there is a *mélange* of architectural influences, ranging from the colonial era through to the Francophilia of the *Porfiriato*, Art Deco, Modernism, the unrefined simplicity of Brutalism, and the International Style. In certain parts this city is sophisticated and modern, but in others it is archaic and neglected. And you can't help but be haunted by its history, with the Aztecs and their own great metropolis now buried beneath a mass of roadways and buildings.

When Cortés ordered the construction of a capital for New Spain built upon the rubble of what had been before his invasion in 1522, it was a powerfully symbolic gesture. But it stored up a mass of problems for the future. The Aztec population lived, worked and developed their environment within a complex maze of waterways and islands spread out upon the lakes and shores of the Valley of Mexico. The new city has periodically suffered from what some argue was too little water and some argue was too much. There have been floods in its history, with water failing to drain properly through the volcanic rock, but the city has also been gradually sinking into the old lake bed and slipping downwards as the fragile earth below dries and contracts. Many of the older buildings in the centre of the city, including the Cathedral, show signs of this battle with the soil, as they dip and tilt with the shifting foundations.

It has fallen to a new generation of architects to add sense as well as a refreshing, contemporary beauty to the metropolis, which seems so very far removed from the spheres of its coasts and countryside. Alberto Kalach, working with Teodoro González de León and a team of engineers and surveyors, has been developing urban-planning proposals that aim to re-establish some balance between the natural and the urban by protecting and preserving the remaining waterways, while at the same time regenerating neglected parts of the city. It is unclear whether Kalach and others of his generation might ever succeed in their ambitious plans to revitalize the city and re-order its infrastructure. In the meantime,

PREVIOUS PAGES (LEFT)
The sprung-steel staircase in the home, office and studio of architect Agustín Hernández in Lomas, Mexico City (see page 138).
(RIGHT) *A view of the sprawling Mexico City skyline seen from a hillside on the road to Cuernevaca.*
LEFT *A sculptural concrete wall around a lava field at the National University of Mexico (UNAM), Mexico City.*
ABOVE *Murals by David Alfaro Siqueiros, near the World Trade Centre, Mexico City; a street scene outside a church in Cuernevaca; and the Habita Hotel, a feat of glass by TEN Arquitectos, in the capital's Condesa district.*

they have been applying their ideas to individual projects, forging a new identity for neo-Mexican architecture within the hot coals of the metropolis.

These are the heirs of Barragán and Candela, as well as Le Corbusier and Mies van der Rohe. Their frame of reference is wide, stretching back into Mexican history and running the length of Modernism and beyond, with an awareness of global stylistic movements and shifts in technology. Above all, these architects are willing to experiment with materials, engineering and developing ideas, as they guide Mexican contemporary architecture into the twenty-first century. Indeed, the power and accomplishment of contemporary Mexican design is striking and is making its mark both at home and internationally. Yet it still retains a hold on themes that have become familiar throughout the evolution of Mexican architecture. There are persistent echoes of the country's pre-Hispanic and colonial past in the use of materials, colour and texture. There is a love of patios, terraces and spaces that create a fluid, open relationship between inside and out. There is a passion for organic elements, even within the most modern of buildings, inviting nature into the home in the form of water pools, landscaping and gardens that are intrinsic to the design, rather than added as afterthoughts.

As well as metro stations, schools, low-cost housing and apartments, Kalach has designed the GGG House in Mexico City. It is undeniably modern, built largely with concrete and glass, yet even within its city context it manages to form an intimate relationship with the outdoors, and has a garden that helps to enclose and protect this family home from the world beyond. Water pools filled with fish add another natural feature, and towards the top of the house a roof garden with a blaze of heathery grasses introduces highlights of colour. The large, sliding glass doors and windows in the main sitting room bordering the lawns ensure an almost seamless flow between the two zones.

An hour's drive to the south of Mexico City, Kalach's former business partner Daniel Alvarez of Grupo Arquitectura collaborated on a house with owner and interior designer Ezequiel Farca. 'One of the things about being in Mexico City is that you need to escape and isolate yourself,' says Farca, 'so we try to go out to the house every weekend. We had a slim plot of land, so the idea was to create one long, continuous platform with the house, terraces and a 25-metre swimming pool in a line. The climate is very warm, with lots of oranges and jasmine and other fragrant plants. When you swim you get the wonderful aroma of oranges.' It is a refuge from the metropolis, offering a retreat into an enclosed, protected environment encompassing house and garden.

Villa en Verdes in Lomas in Mexico City, designed by Jorge Covarrubias and Benjamin Gonzalez Henze of Celula Arquitectura, also maximizes the connections between the home and the environment. Here there is an internal courtyard that brings light right into the centre of a contemporary space. Most of the key rooms of the house look onto either the courtyard or the surrounding gardens. 'The house is organized in such a way that you do have this strong relationship with nature,' says Covarrubias, 'and we liked the idea that you are interacting with this courtyard in which shadows are always moving and you have a fountain and the sound of the water, which you have to be quiet to hear. It's like a double exercise in patience – one to enjoy the movement of the light, the other to listen to the fountain.'

Considering how introspective and insular much urban architecture can be, particularly so with many period buildings in Mexico City, it is interesting to see how contemporary architects are reinterpreting elements such as the courtyard and the patio, following the example of Barragán, Legorreta and their contemporaries in some respects, but at the same time unafraid to experiment and innovate and create their own identity.

'Mexico does have an impeccable record in modern architecture, from the 1920s onwards', says Bernardo Gomez-Pimienta, who works with Enrique Norten at TEN Arquitectos, one of the most exciting young practices in Mexico today. 'I think we have our roots in Mexican architecture, but our work also comes out of Modernism. There are certain basic elements that go from one of our projects to another, although it's important to us that each building is specific to its location. But there's always a clarity of structure: our buildings are always straightforward and clear in the use of light and we are always interested in the visible aura of the materials we use. They are very honest buildings, where you can really see what's going on.'

TEN Arquitectos has become well known for its willingness to innovate with materials, using glass as both a structural and a decorative tool – employed to dramatic effect at Mexico City's fashionable Habita Hotel – or new elements such as the semi-transparent polycarbon coating used at its Parque España apartment building for Haydeé Rovirosa. Gomez-Pimienta argues that there is no such thing as a good or bad material and no quality scale. Any material can work as long as it is used in the right way.

From Mexico City, TEN has spread its wings to carry out design projects in Budapest and Los Angeles, Texas, Miami and New Mexico, and it has recently been working on a new public library for Brooklyn in New York. It is notable that so many Mexican architects – including TEN, Legorreta, Manolo Mestre, Celula and others – are now in regular demand in the United States, a recognizable trend that is paralleled by the popularity

of Mexican film, art and literature. In Europe, too, and even in Spain, contemporary Mexican architects and designers are making their mark.

The reasons for this are surely to do with the remarkable vibrancy of Mexican architecture, design and decoration. There is such a rich heritage of influences and ideas to call upon in Mexico, alongside an openness to history and modernity, nature and art. Notions and concepts drawn from Spanish, Moorish, Roman, French and Anglo-American roots pass through the filter of Mexican inventiveness, and are then caught and made afresh to produce something new and unique. This is a place where creativity somehow comes naturally, given the sheer variety of inspiration and available resources across this vast and endlessly surprising country. Mexico is at an exciting and influential time in its life. It is undoubtedly the perfect moment to explore this most intoxicating and colourful of places.

ABOVE *The fish market at Mercado Abastos, Mexico City. Much of the city's fresh fruit, vegetables, meat and fish filters through this great complex of modern market buildings.*

LEFT AND RIGHT 'The setting here was very important,' says architect Alberto Kalach. 'In this case, the location wasn't that interesting because there is an apartment building behind and an entrance to a golf club on the other side. So we decided to make the house introverted, just like a labyrinth, with its own private patios and gardens.' A view from the rear of the house shows the way it folds in upon itself, with its exposed outward face preserving the privacy of the owners, while on the ground level a water pool, filled with fish, casts reflections and light onto the house (left). Internal glass and skylights cut into the structure of the house and send light coursing through the rooms (right).

GGG HOUSE

Alberto Kalach describes the GGG House as a 'friendly labyrinth'. The site and views in this Mexico City neighbourhood were uninspiring and awkward, so Kalach created an introspective design that used the integrated garden as a natural barrier, protecting and caressing the house, which was built for an entrepreneur and his family.

'It was important that the house be family friendly,' says Kalach. 'I've heard that it is a fun place for the kids, because labyrinths always are. We had the idea of the labyrinth and then the client mentioned that he liked concrete. We saw that this would be the perfect material to give continuity to the house and allow us to do almost anything with the structure.'

The concrete walls are purposefully imperfect and textured, suggesting the concept behind the house's construction and reinforcing its character, almost like adobe. The concrete was softened with materials such as travertine and wood, while glass is incorporated in many ways, including the use of an internal glazed bridge upstairs.

Despite the monumentality expressed by the concrete, the glass and a fluid, yet complex, floor plan provides a feeling of openness. Within the house there are striking contrasts between more enclosed private spaces and generously proportioned rooms. 'Sometimes you need privacy and sometimes a connection with outside,' says Kalach.

At the heart of the house is a sculpture by Jorge Yazpik, a good friend of the architect. 'He helped me to understand space in a different way. As a sculptor he has a different approach to space, taking away elements piece by piece, quite unlike the architect's additive approach.'

ABOVE AND RIGHT *The concrete inside the house retains the marks and textures of the process used in its construction. Like adobe, it has a raw, intrinsic beauty of its own. It also provides a neutral backdrop for a collection of modern art and the occasional antique. In more exposed areas, such as the hallway alcove with a small shrine-like corner (above far right), small windows are cut into the concrete, allowing light to filter in. Other parts of the house feature large, sliding glass doors that open onto the gardens.*

LEFT AND ABOVE *'I draw on a wide palette of materials,' says Kalach, 'but I don't think much about style. I think about solving a problem, about space, light, materials and how this building is going to be constructed.' Here the materials tie the artificiality of concrete to natural materials such as walnut woodwork and sheets of onyx used in windows to introduce some small explosions of coloured light (left). 'We saw that concrete was the perfect material to give continuity to the house and it allows you to have bigger overhangs, to do almost anything. But then we used wood to create the softer parts of the house, and also travertine for the ground floor spaces, which are more in contact with the exteriors.'*

LEFT AND RIGHT *'One of the main things for me in designing the apartment was light,' says Haydeé Rovirosa. 'When the architects saw the site, they said it's perfectly oriented so you will have light all day long. And the park, of course, is so beautiful, so they proposed the terraces at the front of the building.' A view of the stairway from the mezzanine sitting room (left) reveals the volume of the front section of the penthouse with its double-height space, the balcony beyond, and then the park. The majority of the furniture is Italian, including the dining table and chairs from B&B Italia.*

PARQUE ESPAÑA

There are not that many parks in Mexico City. So when you find yourself close to one, you need to make the most of it. That was certainly true of Haydeé Rovirosa – gallery owner, patron of the arts and entrepreneur – when she developed a new building that included a penthouse apartment for herself at Parque España in Condesa with Bernardo Gomez-Pimienta and Enrique Norten of TEN Arquitectos.

Here the park becomes a garden, with the public face of the penthouse looking out across the trees and greenery. At the front of the apartment, the feeling is very open with a double-height space encompassing sitting and dining areas, while the bedrooms and service rooms are tucked away to the rear. Stairs take you up to a galleried area holding a more intimate lounge and also a study to one side with further rooms beyond.

'It is a fantastic site,' says Gomez-Pimienta, 'and the idea was to respond to the location. You have small balconies at the side and large terraces at the front. We are also creating a roof garden for the whole building, which will provide this platform overlooking the park.'

Using glass and a layer of polycarbon strips at one side, the design of the building plays games with light. Rich in daylight, the character of the penthouse changes as the sun moves across the sky. 'At dawn the building seems to explode with colour,' says Gomez-Pimienta. 'Sometimes it seems very solid and at other times almost transparent.' Rovirosa has her gallery on the ground floor and Norten loved the building so much that he took an apartment there himself.

ABOVE AND LEFT The side balcony (above left and right), lined by the layers of polycarbon strips on the outside of the building and the blinds inside. Together they indulge in games with light as the sun takes its course through the day. The front balcony features artwork by Gabriel Orozco while for the inside Haydeé commissioned the large tree-like mural from Pablo Vargas Lugo. The coffee table is by Cappellini and the sofa and chair are from B&B Italia (left).

RIGHT Service areas like the kitchen are tucked away to the rear of the apartment (above left), while the bedrooms are also to the rear on both levels (below left and right). In one bedroom a B&B Italia recliner sits next to a bed with a glass headboard designed by Bernardo Gomez-Pimienta. On the mezzanine gallery (above right), which leads to the bedrooms and bathrooms at the rear, there is a smaller, more intimate lounge and a built-in study and office area, which makes maximum use of the available space.

VILLA EN VERDES

Jorge Covarrubias and Benjamin Gonzalez Henze of Celula Arquitectura both worked for a time as members of the Legorreta & Legorreta design team before setting up their own practice. Luis Barragán was also a strong influence, especially as a magical creator of calming atmospheres and moods. Yet since they joined forces in 1998, they have delivered individual projects with very strong identities of their own.

Villa en Verdes in Mexico City reflects their particular concern with relating a house to its environment and to nature. Its central courtyard and landscaped gardens include a striking series of water pools with striped, multi-coloured, mosaic bases, which surround much of the house like a moat, even completed with a wooden footbridge.

'Barragán used to say that water brings us peace, joy and sensuality,' says Covarrubias. 'We certainly go along with that. The most important idea for the house was to create an atmosphere of serenity.'

Marble in a warm, soothing tone was used to coat and unify the house, a material that will be enriched with time, and one that offers a fine, neutral canvas for the client's collection of artwork. Parota, a tropical wood from the coast, was chosen as a visual and sensory contrast for doorways and ceiling panels and in areas such as the dramatic bar, where Celula collaborated with an artist to create a striking, abstract backdrop.

'When we design a house, it's like making a movie,' says Covarrubias. 'We create a concept that directs you through the house so that you are always discovering something new.'

LEFT, BELOW LEFT AND BELOW *The sitting room leads to a large, rectangular courtyard (left); the sliding wooden door is made to Celula's design (below left); the bar area (below), with its colourful, garden-like graphics was designed with artist Antonio Sanchez, while the bar itself is made with parota, a tropical hardwood.*

RIGHT AND FAR RIGHT *The main courtyard at the centre of the house, with areas for dining and eating (right). This is a highly flexible space, with sliding glass doors to the sitting room and a moving screen at ceiling height that can be adjusted to provide shade. A courtyard centre point is highly traditional, as in Spanish and Moorish architecture, yet it has been updated in this most contemporary of homes. Beyond is another view of the sitting room (far right, above), revealing its collection of Mexican paintings, and a detail of the courtyard seating area (far right, below).*

CASA FARCA

As an interior and furniture designer, Ezequiel Farca is used to working with some of Mexico's brightest contemporary architects. Yet his collaboration with Daniel Alvarez on a new house in the Tepoztlan Valley, to the south of Mexico City, was a more personal affair. Together they fashioned a home for Farca and his wife, Mónica Calderón, a designer with her own homeware collection.

'Tepoztlan is a unique place,' says Farca, who has a furniture and interiors store called Unika in Mexico City. 'The legends say it's a landing site for UFOs. One time we were leaving the valley at night and saw flashes in the sky. The guardian of the house told us it was our goodbye sign. He was very serious.'

The Farcas found a slim plot of land with views of the surrounding mountains, a location wrapped in nature. They wanted a low-maintenance retreat, a simple but contemporary home that made the most of its surroundings. Together with Alvarez they created a unique domestic and outdoor space, which was largely prefabricated in Mexico City and then pieced together on site just like a huge jigsaw puzzle.

'The idea was to use these very raw and natural materials,' says Farca. 'The base and floors are concrete and the supporting steel structures are very visible. The two main walls, surrounded by glass, look as if they are floating. That was Daniel's concept – a floating house.' The interior follows the theme of simplicity and transparency with no curtains, no doors, no handrails for the stairs. Above all, the terraces and decks are treated as outdoor rooms, always in use.

ABOVE AND RIGHT *Much of the furniture in the house is by Ezequiel Farca and his company Unika, and it tends to evolve and change. The low cut-away glass walls to the sides with concrete slabs on the steel frame above create the impression that the house is floating a few feet above ground.*

ABOVE AND RIGHT 'One of the things about being in Mexico City is that you need to escape and isolate yourself every now and then,' says Farca. 'We try to go out to the house every weekend and sometimes stay out there and work. The location was very important for us – it's very open with wonderful views. And the idea was to have these very raw and natural materials. So you can be there and not worry about cleaning or looking after things. Everything is as it is.'

DIRECTORY

ARCHITECTS/DESIGNERS

Daniel Alvarez
Grupo Arquitectura, Colonia
Nochebuena, Mexico D.F., 03720,
Mexico
T + 52 555 563 1589
T + 52 555 563 7765
daf@grupoarquitectura.com

Margarita M Alvarez
Diseno de Interiores, San Carlos
12, San Angel, Mexico D.F., 01020,
Mexico
T + 52 555 500 8948
F + 52 555 550 6911
margaritamalvarez@yahoo.
com.mx

Monica Calderón
Campos Eliseos 158, Colonia
Polanco, Mexico D.F., 11560,
Mexico
T + 52 555 254 1625
unika@prodigy.net.mx

Celula Arquitectura
Campos Eliseos 432, Colonia
Polanco, Mexico D.F., 11560,
Mexico
T + 52 555 281 7640
F + 52 555 281 7641
jcb@celulaarquitectura.com
www.celulaarquitectura.com

Nicole Dugal
PO Box 33, Zihuatanejo,
Guerrero, 40880, Mexico
T + 52 755 553 2863
F + 52 755 553 2867

Duccio Ermenegildo
345 East 56th Street, Apt.16G,
New York, NY, 10022
T + 1 212 754 2621
deremenegildo@compuserve.
com

Ezequiel Farca
Unika, Campos Eliseos 158,
Colonia Polanco, Mexico D.F.,
11560, Mexico
T + 52 555 254 1625
T + 52 555 250 0896
F + 52 555 255 3688
ezequiel@unika.com.mx
www.unika.com.mx

Teodoro González de León
Amsterdam 63, Mexico D.F.,
06100, Mexico
T + 52 555 286 5460
T + 52 555 286 5578
F + 52 555 211 3706
teog@data.net.mx

Agustín Hernández
Bosque de Acacias No. 61,
Colonia Bosques de las Lomas,
Mexico D.F., 11020, Mexico
T + 52 555 596 1665
T + 52 555 596 1065
F + 52 555 596 1710
augustinhdez@infosel.net.mx

Alberto Kalach
Filomeno Mata 11-1, Centro
Historico, Mexico D.F., 06000,
Mexico
T + 52 555 512 2500
F + 52 555 512 2777
alberto@kalach.com
www.kalach.com

Legorreta & Legorreta
Palacio de Versalles 285-A, Mexico
D.F., 11020, Mexico
T + 52 555 251 9698
F + 52 555 596 6162

Manolo Mestre
Parque Via Reforma 2009, Mexico
D.F., 11000, Mexico
T + 52 555 596 9545
F + 52 555 251 2498
mmestre@mail.internet.com.mx

Alex Possenbacher
Apartado No. 29, San Pattricio,
Melaque, Jalisco, 48980, Mexico
T + 52 315 351 0164
F + 52 315 351 0298
apossenbacher@prodigy.net.mx

TEN Arquitectos
Cuernavaca 114-PB, Colonia
Condesa, Mexico D.F., 06140,
Mexico
T + 52 555 211 8004
F + 52 555 286 1735

Hector Velazquez Graham
Despacho de Arquitectos, Atlanta
143 – PB, Colonia Nochebuena,
Mexico D.F., 03720, Mexico
T + 52 555 563 4979
F + 52 555 563 0620

De Yturbe Arquitectos
Sierra Mojada 626-2, Lomas de
Barrilaco, Mexico D.F., 11010,
Mexico
T + 52 555 540 4368
T + 52 555 540 4398
F + 52 555 520 8621

ACCOMMODATION

Bleu & Blanc
Petits Hotels, Paseo de la Reforma
2625-bis, Colonia Lomas Altas,
Mexico D.F., 11950, Mexico
T + 52 559 149 9700
F + 52 555 257 4185
www.bblanc.com

Camino Real
Mariano Escobedo 700, México
D.F., 11590, Mexico
T + 52 555 263 8888
F + 52 555 250 6897
mex@caminoreal.com
www.caminoreal.com/mexico

Cuixmala
Costa Careyes, Jalisco, Mexico
*For details of house rentals, contact
Maria Campos*
T + 52 315 351 0044
F + 52 315 351 0040
ecamposl@prodigy.net.mx

Design Hotels
T 0800 169 8817 (UK)
T 800 337 4685 (USA)
www.designhotels.com

Habita Hotel
Av. Presidente Masaryk 201,
Colonia Polanco, Mexico D.F.,
11560, Mexico
T + 52 555 282 3100
F + 52 555 282 3101
info@hotelhabita.com
www.hotelhabita.com
www.designhotels.com
www.bblanc.com

Hacienda San José Cholul
(Grupo Plan), Tixkokob,
Yucatán, 97800, Mexico
T + 52 555 257 0097
F + 52 555 257 0151
info@grupoplan.com
www.grupoplan.com
www.bblanc.com

Hacienda Santa Rosa
(Grupo Plan), Maxcanú, Yucatán,
97805, Mexico
T + 52 555 257 0097
F + 52 555 257 0151
info@grupoplan.com
www.grupoplan.com
www.bblanc.com

Hacienda Uayamón
(Grupo Plan), Campeche,
24530, Mexico
T + 52 555 257 0097
F + 52 555 257 0151
info@grupoplan.com
www.grupoplan.com
www.bblanc.com

Hotel Careyes
(Grupo Plan), Costa Careyes,
Las Huertas, Jalisco, 48970,
Mexico
T + 52 555 257 0097
F + 52 555 257 0151
info@grupoplan.com
www.grupoplan.com
www.bblanc.com

Hotel Deseo
5a Av. y Calle 12, Playa del
Carmen, Quintana Roo,
77710, Mexico
T + 52 984 879 3620
F + 52 984 879 3621
info@hoteldeseo.com
www.hoteldeseo.com
www.designhotels.com
www.bblanc.com

Hotelito Desconocido
La Cruz de Loreto, Tomatlan,
Jalisco, Mexico
Carr. a Mismaloya 479-205,
Edificio Scala, Puerto Vallarata,
Jalisco, 48380, Mexico
T + 52 322 222 2526
F + 52 322 223 0293
hotelito@hotelito
www.hotelito.com
www.slh.com

Ikal del Mar
Fraccíon 7, Manzana 20, Colonia
Xcalacoco, Municipio de
Solidaridad Playa del Carmen,
Quintana Roo, 77710, Mexico
T + 52 984 877 3000
T 00800 525 48000
F + 52 984 877 3009
info@ikaldelmar.com
www.ikaldelmar.com
www.slh.com/ikaldelmar

**Mahakua, Hacienda de
San Antonio**
Municipio de Comala, Colima,
28450, Mexico
T + 52 312 313 4411
F + 52 312 314 3727
hacienda@mahakua.com.mx
www.amanresorts.com

**Small Luxury Hotels of
the World**
T 00800 525 48000 (UK)
T 800 525 4800 (USA)
www.slh.com

Verana
Puerto Vallarta, Jalisco, 48319,
Mexico
T + 52 322 227 5420
T + 1 800 677 5156
www.verana.com

MEXICAN TRAVEL

British Airways
T 0845 773 3377
www.ba.com

Cathy Matos Mexican Tours
75 St Margaret's Avenue,
Whetstone, London, N20 9LD
T 020 8492 0000
F 020 8446 4044
sales@mextours.co.uk
www.cathymatosmexico.com

Mexicana
75 St Margaret's Avenue,
Whetstone, London,
N20 9LD
T 020 8492 0000
F 020 8446 4044
sales@mextours.co.uk
www.mexicana.com

Luis Miguel López Alanís
Tour Guide, Mex Mich Guías
Turismo Personalizado, Antonia
Morelos 262, Inf. Juana Pavón,
Morelia, Michoacán, Mexico
T + 52 443 320 1157
mexmich@prodigy.net.mx
www.mmg.com.mx

INDEX

Figures in *italics* indicate captions.

ACKNOWLEDGEMENTS

The publishers and authors would like to thank the owners, designers and architects of the houses, hotels and studios featured for their kindness and hospitality:

Daniel Alvarez, Margarita M Alvarez, Dr Sabino Yano Bretón, Paz Virginia Yano Bretón, Gian Franco Brignone, James and Alexandra Brown, Monica Calderón, Enrique Martin-Moreno Cerrancedo, Jorge Covarrubias, Nicole Dugal, Ezequiel Farca, Plutarco Gastelum, the GGG family, Bernardo Gomez-Pimienta, Laura Laviada, Hector Velazquez Graham, Benjamin Gonzalez Henze, Grupo Plan and Roberto Hernández, Agustin Hernández, Sergio Hernández, Alberto Kalach, Heinz Legler, Ricardo Legorreta, Victor Legorreta, Veronique Lievre, Teodoro González de León, Alix and Goffredo Marcaccini, Ramón Torres Martinéz, the Mascarenas family, Manolo Mestre, Marcello Murzilli, Enrique Norten, Alejandro Patron, Alex and Lorena Possenbacher, Michael and Nicolette Possenbacher, Haydeé Rovirosa, the Tribull family, José de Yturbe, the guardians of Capilla de Tlalpan and Santo Domingo and the owners of Casa Galves, Casa del Sabino, Casa Vigil, San Cristóbal, Casa en el Aire and Villa en Verdes.

The authors would also like to thank the following for their assistance:

Luis Miguel López Alanís, Valter Bosterley, Faith, Florence and Cecily Bradbury, Daisy Bridgewater, British Airways, Isaac Broid, Kate Chesshyre and Design Hotels, Catalina Corcquera, Avery and Lenore Danziger, Arely Diaz, Duccio Ermenegildo, John Finnerty, Charlotte Fraser, Carlos Fuentes, Sara Topelson de Gainberg, Isabel Grangen, Claire Gray, Henry and Char Grey, Karen Howes, Gwen Jones, Naihala Lasharie, Charlotte Martins and Small Luxury Hotels, Cathy Matos, Joanne Matos, Nicolle Aimee Meyer, Aurora Lopez de Ortigosa, Carmen Parra, Emiliano Parra, Jonny Pegg, Claudia Raimondi, Carla Rinetti and Blanc and Bleu, Pedro and Carla Diego Rivera, Americo Sanchez, Claudia Silva, Rafael Micha Smeke, Frederico Spada, Andrew and Camille de Stempel, Francisco Toledo, Isabella Tree, Corinthia West, Federica Zanco and Instituto Nacional de Antropología e Historia (www.inah.gob.mx).

And thanks to all at Conran Octopus: Lorraine Dickey, Chi Lam, Zia Mattocks, Alison Fenton, Liz Boyd, Emma Clegg and Angela Couchman.

With special thanks to Dominique Colliere, Edouard Labouret, Alix and Goffredo Marcaccini, and Leo Martinez.

Painting by Pedro Diego Rivera

SELECT BIBLIOGRAPHY

Mario A Arnaboldi, preface, *González de Leon: Architecture as Art*, L'Arca Edizioni, 1998

René Burri, *Luis Barragán* Phaidon, 2000

John Collis and David M Jones, *Mexico Blue Guide*, A & C Black, 1996

Hernán Cortés, *Letters from Mexico*, Yale University Press, 1986

Bernal Díaz, *The Conquest of New Spain*, Penguin, 1973

Victoria Finlay, *Colour: Travels Through the Paintbox*, Sceptre, 2002

Carlos Fuentes, *A New Time for Mexico*, University of California Press, 1997; *The Buried Mirror: Reflections on Spain and the New World*, Peter Smith, 1999; *The Death of Artemio Cruz*, Farrar, Straus & Giroux, 1991

Graham Greene, *The Lawless Roads*, Vintage, 2002

D H Lawrence, *Mornings in Mexico*, Penguin, 1986

Malcolm Lowry, *Under The Volcano*, Penguin, 1962

Patrick Maher, *Mexico Handbook: The Travel Guide*, Footprint Handbooks, 2000

John Mutlow, ed., *Ricardo Legorreta Architects*, Rizzoli, 1997

Octavio Paz, *The Labyrinth of Solitude and Other Writings*, Grove Press, 1985

Kenneth Pearce, *A Traveller's History of Mexico*, Cassell & Co., 2002

Chloë Sayer, *Arts and Crafts of Mexico*, Thames & Hudson, 1989

Hugh Thomas, *The Conquest of Mexico*, Hutchinson, 1993

Isabella Tree, *Sliced Iguana: Travels in Mexico*, Penguin, 2002

Villela, Bradbury & Wagner, *Contemporary Mexican Design and Architecture*, Gibbs Smith, 2003

Mariana Yampolsky & Chloë Sayer, *The Traditional Architecture of Mexico*, Thames & Hudson, 1994

Federica Zanco, ed., *Luis Barragán: The Quiet Revolution*, Skira, 2001